Frozen SWEET TREATS & DESSERTS

OVER 70 RECIPES FOR POPSICLES, SUNDAES, SHAKES, FLOATS & ICE CREAM CAKES

RYLAND PETERS & SMALL
LONDON • NEW YORK

Senior Designer Megan Smith
Editorial Director Julia Charles
Creative Director Leslie Harrington
Head of Production Patricia Harrington

Indexer Vanessa Bird

Note: The recipes in this book have been previously published by Ryland Peters & Small. See page 160 for full details.

First published in 2023 by
Ryland Peters & Small
20–21 Jockey's Fields
London WC1R 4BW
and Ryland Peters & Small, Inc.
341 East 116th Street
New York NY 10029

www.rylandpeters.com

Text © Hannah Miles, Louise Pickford, Victoria Glass, Ryland Peters & Small 2023
Design and photographs © Ryland Peters & Small 2023

ISBN: 978-1-78879-514-2

10 9 8 7 6 5 4 3 2 1

Printed and bound in China

CIP data from the Library of Congress has been applied for. A CIP record for this book is available from the British Library.

NOTES
* Both British (metric) and American (imperial plus US cups) are included; however, its important not to alternate between the two within a recipe.
* All spoon measurements are level unless specified otherwise.
* All eggs are medium (UK) or large (US), unless specified as large, in which case US extra large should be used. Uncooked or partially cooked eggs should not be served to the very old, frail, young children, pregnant women or those with compromised immune systems.
* Ovens should be preheated to the specified temperatures. If using a fan-assisted oven, adjust according to the manufacturer's instructions.
* When a recipe calls for the grated zest of citrus fruit, buy unwaxed fruit and wash well before using. If you can only find treated fruit, scrub well in warm soapy water before using.

CONTENTS

No matter how old you are, there are few things more tempting than a neon-bright frozen popsicle, a frothy milkshake in a frosted glass, or an ice cream sundae loaded with fruit, whipped cream and nuts. This delightful book brings you all manner of fun and retro frozen treats, from simple soft whips to showstopping baked Alaska. Choose from fresh and fruity, or rich and decadent – there is something here for every taste and occasion!

Many of the recipes use store-bought ice cream and sauces so if you are short on time, buy in good-quality ready-made tubs and cartons and create frozen magic in an instant! If you do have more time making your own delicious ice creams and sorbets at home is a relatively easy process. There are many types of ice cream machines available; some contain a freezer unit which enables you to churn ice cream almost instantly – others have a freezer bowl that requires you to freeze it for about 6–8 hours. And if you don't not have a machine, don't worry! Simply place your mixture in a lidded freezerproof box and pop it in the freezer. Remove from the freezer every hour or so, transfer to a large bowl and whisk with an electric handmixer to incorporate air, break up ice crystals and give a light texture. Repeat every hour until your ice cream is completely frozen.

The COLD, the SWEET & the CREAMY...

This basic recipe is used throughout the book and, with the addition of whatever ingredients you choose to add, you can create a wonderful array of interesting flavours. This makes about 650 ml/2¾ cups of ice cream.

VANILLA *ice cream*

1 vanilla pod/bean
200 ml/¾ cup whole milk
400 ml/1⅔ cups double/heavy cream
100 g/½ cup caster/white granulated sugar
5 egg yolks

Split the vanilla pod/bean in half lengthways and then run the back of the knife along the length of each half of the pod/bean to remove the black seeds. Place the seeds, pod halves, milk and cream in a heavy-based pan and bring to the boil. Immediately remove from the heat and leave to infuse for 15–20 minutes. Meanwhile whisk together the sugar and egg yolks until light and creamy and doubled in size. Remove the vanilla pod/bean, bring the mixture to the boil again and then, while still whisking, slowly pour in the hot vanilla cream. Return the custard mixture to the pan and over a gentle heat, whisk for a few minutes until the mixture begins to thicken. Set aside until the mixture has cooled completely, then transfer to the fridge to chill. When chilled, add any additional flavourings to the base and churn in an ice cream machine until frozen (according to the machine manufacturer's instructions), or alternatively you can freeze using the by-hand method given on page 6.

STRAWBERRY

Prepare the Vanilla Ice Cream base according to the method given left. Let cool then blitz in a blender until smooth with 400 g/14 oz. hulled fresh strawberries and a few drops of pink food colouring (optional). Churn or freeze as in main recipe.

CHOCOLATE

Prepare the Vanilla Ice Cream base according to the method given left. Let cool then stir in 200 g/7 oz. melted dark chocolate. Churn or freeze as in main recipe.

These sauces can all be stored in the refrigerator for a few days. For most of the recipes in this book, the sauces should be cooled completely before using, however they can be served warm over any ice cream for an instant sundae.

Simple SAUCES

CHOCOLATE

2 tablespoons golden/light corn syrup
100 ml/⅓ cup plus 1 tablespoon double/heavy cream
100 g/3½ oz. dark chocolate
30 g/¼ stick unsalted butter

MAKES 300 ML/1¼ CUPS

Place all the ingredients together in a heavy-based pan and whisk over a gentle heat until the chocolate has melted and the sauce is smooth and glossy.

TOFFEE CARAMEL

80 g/scant ½ cup light brown sugar
40 g/¼ cup dark brown sugar
200 ml/¾ cup double/heavy cream
60 g/½ stick unsalted butter
1 tablespoon golden/light corn syrup

MAKES 415 ML/1¾ CUPS

Place all the ingredients together in a heavy-based saucepan and whisk over gentle heat until the butter has melted, the sugar dissolved and the sauce is smooth and thick.

SUMMER BERRY

1 vanilla pod/bean or 1 teaspoon vanilla extract
250 g/9 oz. fresh strawberries, hulled
150 g/5¼ oz. fresh raspberries
100 g/1 cup caster/superfine sugar

MAKES 500 ML/2 CUPS

Cut the vanilla pod/bean in half lengthways. Place all the ingredients in a pan with 200 ml/¾ cup water and simmer for 8–10 minutes, until the strawberries are very soft and the sugar has dissolved. Strain through a fine mesh sieve/strainer, pressing the fruit down with the back of a spoon. Discard the fruit.

Shakes & FLOATS

Rich caramel banana milk – this drink is an absolute must for banana lovers, and in particular fans of banoffee pie. If you are not able to find banana-flavoured ice cream, you can substitute store-bought or homemade vanilla ice cream (see page 8) for equally delicious results.

BANANA CARAMEL
shake

4 tablespoons toffee caramel sauce (see page 9), plus extra to drizzle

2 ripe bananas, peeled and sliced

500 ml/2 cups milk, chilled

4 scoops store-bought banana ice cream, or vanilla ice cream (see page 8)

a few drops of yellow food colouring (optional)

2 dried banana chips, to decorate

2 soda glasses, chilled

2 paper straws

SERVES 2

Spoon 1 tablespoon of the toffee caramel sauce into each glass and swirl the glass until there is a thin coating of caramel sauce over the bottom half of the glass. This will give a pretty two-tone effect when the shake is poured into the glasses.

Put the bananas in a blender with the milk, 2 tablespoons caramel sauce, 2 scoops of the ice cream and the food colouring, if using, and whizz until very foamy and thick.

Pour the shake into chilled glasses and top with a second scoop of ice cream. Decorate each glass with a dried banana chip and a drizzle of toffee caramel sauce and serve immediately with paper straws.

With Reese's peanut butter chocolates such a popular candy, you can only imagine how delicious this shake is! Rich chocolate syrup, salty peanut butter and a drizzle of toffee caramel, all served ice cold with ice cream – quite simply heaven in a glass! You can use smooth or crunchy peanut butter, whichever you prefer. If you use crunchy, you may want to serve your shakes with a spoon so that you can eat the peanut pieces, which will sink to the bottom of the shake.

PEANUT BUTTER
shake

2 tablespoons chocolate sauce (see page 9)
4 tablespoons toffee caramel sauce (see page 9)
500 ml/2 cups milk, chilled
100 g/½ cup peanut butter, crunchy or smooth, as preferred
4 scoops vanilla ice cream (see page 8)
10 g/1 tablespoon honey roasted peanuts, chopped, to decorate

2 soda glasses, chilled
a squeezy bottle (optional)
2 paper straws

SERVES 2

Drizzle alternating lines of chocolate syrup and caramel sauce down the inside of each glass using a squeezy bottle or a spoon (use about 1 tablespoon of each sauce per glass).

Add the remaining 2 tablespoons of caramel sauce to a blender with the milk, peanut butter and 2 scoops of ice cream and whizz until very foamy and thick.

Pour the shake into the prepared glasses, top each with a scoop of ice cream and sprinkle with the peanuts. Serve immediately with straws.

Chocolate malt shakes are an all-time classic. There is something very comforting about the flavour of malt – think of the warm, malted drinks often given to children at bedtime. This one is topped with malted chocolate-covered balls and served with chocolate ice cream, yum yum!

CHOCOLATE MALT
shake

**4 tablespoons chocolate sauce
(see page 9)**
500 ml/2 cups milk, chilled
**30 g/1 oz. malted milk powder
(such as Horlicks)**
**4 scoops chocolate ice cream
(see page 8)**
**10 milk chocolate-coated malted
milk balls (such as Maltesers),
to decorate**

2 soda glasses, chilled
*a squeezy bottle or piping/pastry
bag with a small round nozzle/tip*

SERVES 2

Put 2 tablespoons of the chocolate sauce in a squeezy bottle or piping/pastry bag and drizzle pretty patterns of sauce up the inside of each glass.

Put the milk in a blender with the malted milk powder, 2 scoops of the ice cream and the remaining chocolate sauce. Whizz until very foamy and thick.

Cut the malted milk balls in half using a sharp knife. Pour the shake into the prepared glasses, top each with a scoop of chocolate ice cream and decorate with the malted milk balls. Serve immediately.

Apple snow is a creamy apple mousse dessert made with whipped cream and apple purée/sauce. It is best made with whipped egg white for lightness, but this can be omitted if you are serving the shake to people who cannot eat raw egg (see note on page 4).

Apple snow SHAKE

APPLE SNOW
**2 green apples, peeled, cored
and thinly sliced**
freshly squeezed juice of ½ lemon
**30 g/2½ tablespoons caster/white
granulated sugar**
150 ml/⅔ cup double/heavy cream
1 egg white

APPLE SLUSHIE
200 ml/¾ cup cloudy apple juice
10 ice cubes
green sugar sprinkles, to decorate
apple slices, to decorate

2 sundae coupes, chilled

SERVES 2

Put the apple slices in a heavy-based pan with the lemon juice, sugar and 3 tablespoons water, and simmer until the apple is very soft. Leave to cool, then purée using a stick blender.

In a large mixing bowl, whip the cream to stiff peaks. In a separate bowl, whip the egg white to stiff peaks. Fold the egg white and apple purée into the whipped cream and store in the refrigerator until needed.

For the apple slushie, put the apple juice and ice cubes in a blender and whizz until the ice is crushed. If your blender is not strong enough to crush ice, place the ice cubes in a plastic bag, seal and wrap in a clean dish towel, and bash the bag with a rolling pin until the ice is crushed. Then add to the blender with the apple juice and blend.

Pour the apple slushie into chilled glasses and top with a spoonful of the apple snow. Decorate with sprinkles and apple slices and serve immediately with small spoons.

Chocolate-covered honeycomb/sponge candy bubbles, which have a brittle crunch when you bite, are the centrepiece of this delicious caramel-flavoured shake. If you can't find honeycomb ice cream, look out for honeycomb choc ices or substitute store-bought or home-made vanilla ice cream (see page 8) and add a little extra candy to the shake.

Honeycomb SHAKE

4 scoops store-bought honeycomb ice cream, or vanilla ice cream (see page 8)
500 ml/2 cups milk
40 g/1½ oz. chocolate-covered honeycomb/sponge candy, roughly chopped

2 soda glasses, chilled
2 paper straws

SERVES 2

Put 2 scoops of the ice cream in a blender with the milk and three-quarters of the chocolate-covered honeycomb/sponge candy, and blitz until thick and creamy.

Pour the shake into the chilled glasses, top each glass with a second scoop of ice cream and sprinkle with the remaining chopped honeycomb/sponge candy. Serve immediately with straws.

Cookies and cream – the popular ice cream flavour – is the inspiration for this indulgent shake. Packed full of Oreo cookies and served with extra cookies on the side, it is naughty but oh, so nice.

Cookies & cream
SHAKE

4 scoops store-bought cookies-and-cream ice cream, or vanilla ice cream (see page 8)

400 ml/1⅔ cups milk

2 tablespoons chocolate sauce (see page 9)

8 Oreo cookies, plus extra to serve

canned whipped fresh cream

2 soda glasses, chilled

SERVES 2

Put 2 scoops of the ice cream in a blender with the milk, chocolate sauce and 7 of the Oreo cookies and whizz until foamy and thick.

Pour into the chilled glasses and top each with a further scoop of ice cream. Squirt a small amount of cream on top of each shake.

Crush the remaining Oreo cookie and sprinkle over the shakes. Serve immediately with more Oreos on the side with long-handled spoons.

Lemon meringue pie is such a beloved retro dessert: the combination of light caramelized meringue and tangy lemon cream is just delicious! This is a shake version: a lemon yogurt drink, topped with a crisp delicate meringue. Serve with a spoon so that you can eat the meringue when you have finished the drink.

LEMON MERINGUE
shake

3 tablespoons lemon curd
300 ml/1¼ cups lemon-
flavoured yogurt
3 scoops store-bought lemon ice
cream or lemon sorbet
300 ml/1¼ cups milk, chilled
2 mini meringues

2 soda glasses, chilled
a squeezy bottle or piping/pastry
bag with a small round
nozzle/tip
2 paper straws

SERVES 2

Put 2 tablespoons of the lemon curd in a squeezy bottle or piping/pastry bag and pipe a lemon spiral onto the inside of each glass.

Put the yogurt, ice cream, milk and remaining tablespoon of lemon curd in a blender and whizz until smooth.

Pour into the prepared glasses and top each with a meringue. Serve immediately with straws and a spoon to eat the meringue.

Chocolate and cherry are an indulgent combination and this delicious drink is no exception. Thick chocolate sauce and frozen cherry yogurt are topped up with fresh cherry juice, which is available in most supermarkets and health food stores. This version is decorated with a whole cherry or, for a special treat, you could use a classic cerisette (chocolate-coated cherries with kirsch).

CHOCOLATE CHERRY *freeze*

2 tablespoons chocolate sauce (see page 9)
250 ml/1 cup cherry juice
2 scoops cherry frozen yogurt
canned whipped fresh cream
chocolate sprinkles, to decorate
2 whole cherries, to decorate

2 tall, stemmed glasses, chilled

SERVES 2

Spoon a tablespoon of chocolate sauce into each glass and swirl so that the bottom third of the glass is coated with syrup.

Put the cherry juice and frozen yogurt in a blender and blitz until frothy. Pour into the prepared glasses and top each with a squirt of whipped cream. Decorate the glasses with chocolate sprinkles and a whole cherry and serve immediately.

Milk, maple syrup and popcorn – could you ask for anything more in a shake? If you're having a 4th July or cheerleading party, why not thread the popcorn onto foil sparkler wands to add a bit of razzle dazzle to your drinks?

MAPLE POPCORN
shake

40 g/1½ oz. caramel-coated popcorn (such as Butterkist)
4 scoops store-bought praline-and-cream ice cream, or vanilla ice cream (see page 9)
2 tablespoons maple syrup
400 ml/1⅔ cups milk, chilled

2 thin wooden skewers
2 soda glasses, chilled
2 paper straws

SERVES 2

Thread about 5 popcorn kernels onto each of the skewers and set aside until you are ready to serve. Take care when threading as the popcorn is fragile.

Put the ice cream, maple syrup, milk and the remaining popcorn in a blender and blitz until very foamy and thick.

Pour into chilled glasses and serve immediately with straws and the popcorn skewers.

Adding a pinch of salt to a sticky caramel sauce gives a whole new depth of flavour. Topped with pieces of fudge and packed full of toffee ice cream, this shake is a creamy, caramel dream!

Salted caramel SHAKE

400 ml/1⅔ cups milk, chilled

4 scoops store-bought toffee or caramel ice cream

2 pieces vanilla fudge, cut into small cubes, to decorate

SALTED CARAMEL SAUCE

100 g/½ cup caster/white granulated sugar

50 g/3 tablespoons butter

a pinch of salt

3 tablespoons double/heavy cream

2 soda glasses, chilled

2 paper straws

SERVES 2

To prepare the salted caramel sauce, put the sugar and butter in a small pan and simmer over a gentle heat until the butter has melted and the sugar dissolved. Add the salt and cream and heat for a further few minutes, stirring, until you have a thick sauce. Set aside to cool.

When cooled, spoon a tablespoonful of the caramel sauce into each glass and swirl so that the bottom half of the glass is coated in caramel.

Put the milk into a blender with the remaining caramel sauce (reserving a little for decoration) and 2 scoops of the ice cream, and blitz until smooth and frothy.

Pour the shake into the prepared glasses and top each with a scoop of ice cream. Sprinkle with the fudge pieces, drizzle with the reserved salted caramel sauce and serve immediately with straws.

At a summer dinner party, why not end the meal with a mint chocolate shake? If you want to make more of an impact, you can intensify the green with a little food colouring. Either way, these shakes are the perfect refreshment on a warm evening.

Mint chocolate
SHAKE

4 scoops store-bought mint choc
    chip ice cream
350 ml/1½ cups milk, chilled
a few drops of green food
    colouring (optional)
chocolate sprinkles, to decorate
4 chocolate peppermint sticks
    or squares, to serve (optional)

CHOCOLATE MINT SAUCE
50 g/1½ oz. peppermint-fondant
    filled dark chocolate squares
    (such as After Eights)
2 tablespoons double/heavy cream
1 tablespoon golden/light corn
    syrup

2 soda glasses, chilled
a squeezy bottle or piping/pastry
    bag with a small round nozzle/tip

SERVES 2

To prepare the chocolate mint sauce, put the peppermint-fondant filled dark chocolate squares in a pan with the cream and syrup and simmer over a gentle heat, stirring, until the chocolate has melted and you have a smooth sauce. Set aside to cool.

Put the chocolate mint sauce in a squeezy bottle or piping/pastry bag and drizzle pretty patterns of sauce up the inside of each glass.

Put 2 scoops of the ice cream in a blender with the milk and the food colouring, if using, and blitz until smooth and frothy.

Pour into the prepared glasses, top each with a scoop of ice cream and decorate with chocolate sprinkles. Serve immediately with more chocolate peppermint squares or chocolate peppermint sticks, if using.

This simple shake was inspired by a delicious pistachio shake enjoyed in a Greek island harbour while waiting for a ferry. It is a truly delicious and indulgent drink – perfect for hot days when you would rather be on a beach in Greece! Pistachio syrup is available from online shops and is a pretty way to decorate your shake glasses.

PISTACHIO
shake

6 scoops store-bought pistachio ice cream
400 ml/1⅔ cups milk, chilled
store-bought pistachio syrup, to drizzle (optional)

2 soda glasses, chilled
2 paper straws

SERVES 2

Put the ice cream in a blender with the milk and blitz until foamy and thick.

Decorate the glasses with a swirl of pistachio syrup, if using, then pour in the shake and serve immediately with straws.

The Peach Melba dessert was invented to honour the Australian soprano, Dame Nellie Melba (see also page 90). This quaffable shake version with added peach schnapps will certainly get your tastebuds singing.

PEACH MELBA
boozy shake

1 x 420-g/16-oz. can peach slices in light sugar syrup
200 ml/7 oz. peach schnapps
4 scoops vanilla ice cream (see page 8)
6 tablespoons summer berry sauce (see page 9), made with just raspberries
a handheld electric blender
2 soda glasses, chilled
2 paper straws

SERVES 2

Drain most of the sugar syrup from the peaches and use a handheld electric blender to purée the fruit. Set aside.

Blend together the peach schnapps and vanilla ice cream until smooth and thick. Add the peach purée and stir to combine. Swirl 3 tablespoons of the raspberry sauce around the inside of each glass. Pour over the peach shake at an angle to create an attractive two-tone pattern in the shake and serve immediately.

For full authenticity, use Key limes, which have a higher acidity and are more aromatic than green Persian limes, although these will do the job nicely if that's all you can find.

Key lime pie
BOOZY SHAKE

grated zest and freshly squeezed
   juice of 2 limes, plus extra
   grated zest to garnish
100 ml/3½ oz. vodka
   (or lime vodka)
4 scoops lime ice cream (see below)
100 ml/⅓ cup milk
2 mini meringues
50 g/½ cup digestive biscuit/
   graham cracker crumbs

LIME ICE CREAM
200 ml/¾ cup condensed milk
250 ml/1 cup double/heavy cream
finely grated zest and freshly
   squeezed juice of 2 limes

2 tumblers, chilled

SERVES 2

Begin by preparing the lime ice cream. Whisk all the ingredients together until very thick and transfer to a airtight plastic container. Simply place it in the freezer for at least 6 hours – there's no need to churn it.

For the shake, blend together the lime zest and juice, vodka and ice cream until thick and smooth. Add the milk and blend again.

Divide the shake between the chilled glasses. Add a mini meringue to the top of each shake. Sprinkle with the crushed biscuit/cracker crumbs and a little extra lime zest before serving immediately.

Dance along to the Piña Colada Song, while slurping from hollowed out pineapples filled with these kitsch cocktail shakes. Fresh, sweet and tropical, you won't even need to get caught in the rain to enjoy them!

Piña colada
BOOZY SHAKE

2 small pineapples
1 tablespoon coconut oil
4 scoops coconut ice cream
    (see below)
200 ml/¾ cup coconut cream
150 ml/5 oz. golden rum
50 ml/1¾ oz. coconut-flavoured
    white rum, such as Malibu
maraschino cherries, to serve

COCONUT ICE CREAM
1 quantity vanilla ice cream base
    made without the vanilla pod/
    bean (see page 8)
50 ml/1¾ oz. coconut-flavoured
    white rum, such as Malibu
175 ml/⅔ cup coconut cream

a pineapple corer
2 cocktail umbrellas
2 paper straws

SERVES 2

Begin by making the coconut ice cream or use a good-quality store-bought ice cream. Follow the instructions for making vanilla ice cream on page 8, omitting the vanilla pod/bean and swap half of the cream for coconut cream and add the coconut-flavoured rum.

Slice the top off of each pineapple and reserve to make lids. Use a pineapple corer to remove the flesh of each fruit and pop your pineapple cups in the fridge until needed.

Place the pineapple flesh in a food processor and liquidize. Push the pineapple purée through a fine mesh sieve/strainer and discard any pulp. Blend together 250 ml/1 cup of the resulting pineapple juice with the coconut oil, coconut ice cream, coconut cream, rum and coconut liqueur, until thick and smooth.

Divide the shake between the chilled pineapple cups. Garnish the edge of each pineapple with 2 maraschino cherries pushed onto a cocktail umbrella. Serve immediately.

No British childhood would be complete without these rhubarb and custard boiled candies from the sweet shop/candy store, served up in a striped paper bag. This boozy shake is full of nostalgia for adults only.

Rhubarb & custard
BOOZY SHAKE

300 ml/10 oz. advocaat liqueur
150 ml/5 oz. rhubarb-flavoured vodka
4 scoops vanilla ice cream (see page 8)
100 ml/⅓ cup milk
4 tablespoons rhubarb compote (or good-quality rhubarb jam/jelly)

2 soda glasses, chilled
2 paper straws

SERVES 2

Blend together the advocaat, rhubarb vodka, ice cream, milk and half of the rhubarb compote until smooth and thick.

Place 1 tablespoon of rhubarb compote in the base of each glass and swirl it up the sides. Divide the shake between the two prepared glasses and serve immediately with straws.

There are various claims to the creation of the first ice cream float, the most popular being that a soda seller ran out of ice to chill his sodas and added ice cream to keep his drinks cool. While these may be the simplest of drinks to prepare, they are guaranteed to put a smile on people's faces. You can use any combination of fizzy drink and ice cream (or sorbet) of your choice – half the fun is coming up with new creations. The soda foam disappears quickly so you need to serve these drinks immediately – or why not let your guests pour over the soda themselves?

COKE *float*

**4 scoops vanilla ice cream
(see page 8)
1 teaspoon vanilla extract
500 ml/2 cups cola, chilled**

2 soda glasses, chilled

SERVES 2

Put one scoop of ice cream and ½ teaspoon vanilla extract in the bottom of each glass. Fill each glass with cola and top with a second scoop of ice cream. Serve immediately.

CREAM SODA *float*

**4 scoops lemon ice cream
or sorbet
500 ml/2 cups cream soda, chilled**

2 soda glasses, chilled

SERVES 2

Put one scoop of sorbet in the bottom of each glass. Fill each glass with cream soda and top with a second scoop of sorbet. Serve immediately.

Raspberry Ripple – vanilla ice cream with raspberry sauce running through it – is a popular children's dessert. Combined with raspberry or cherry soda this is the prettiest of drinks – bright pink and decorated with sugar sprinkles. Serve with a spoon for eating the fresh raspberries.

Raspberry ripple
FLOAT

4 scoops store-bought raspberry
   ripple ice cream
10 fresh raspberries
500 ml/2 cups raspberry or cherry
   soda, chilled
pink sprinkles, to decorate
   (optional)

2 soda glasses, chilled
2 paper straws

SERVES 2

Put one scoop of ice cream in the bottom of each glass and divide the raspberries between them.

Top up the glasses with raspberry or cherry soda and finish with a second scoop of ice cream.

Decorate the top with sprinkles, if using, and serve immediately with straws.

This shake is the ultimate pick-me-up – strong coffee and sweet ice cream. Coffee ice cream can sometimes be tricky to find so if it is not available you can replace it with vanilla ice cream (see page 8) and add another shot of espresso instead.

COFFEE FRAPPÉ *float*

2 shots of espresso, cooled
350 ml/1½ cups milk
4 scoops coffee ice cream
15 ice cubes
canned whipped fresh cream
unsweetened cocoa powder,
    for dusting
2 chocolate-coated coffee beans
    or chocolate coffee-bean shaped
    chocolates, to decorate

2 soda glasses, chilled
2 paper straws

SERVES 2

Put the espresso, milk and 2 scoops of coffee ice cream in a blender with the ice cubes and blitz until thick and creamy. If your blender is not strong enough to crush ice, place the ice cubes in a plastic bag, seal and wrap in a clean dish towel, and bash the bag with a wooden rolling pin until the ice is crushed, then add to the blender with the other ingredients and blitz together.

Pour the shake into the chilled glasses and top each glass with a scoop of coffee ice cream. Squirt a little of the cream on top of the shake, dust with cocoa and top with a chocolate coffee bean. Serve immediately with straws.

This jammy float is a real treat, served with mini doughnut/donut skewers on the side. You can either buy packs of mini ones in a supermarket, or even make your own homemade ones, which are wonderful served warm with the cool shake.

Doughnut FLOAT

4 tablespoons strawberry jam/jelly
500 ml/2 cups milk, chilled
4 scoops vanilla ice cream
  (see page 8)
1 teaspoon vanilla extract
6 mini doughnuts, to serve

2 soda glasses, chilled
wooden skewers

SERVES 2

Using a clean pastry brush, brush stripes of strawberry jam/jelly onto the inside edges of the two glasses to decorate (use 1 tablespoon of jam/jelly per glass).

Thread 3 mini doughnuts onto each skewer and set aside until needed.

Put the remaining 2 tablespoons of jam/jelly into a blender with the milk, 2 scoops of ice cream and the vanilla extract, and whizz until foamy and thick. Pass through a sieve/strainer to remove the strawberry seeds.

Return the shake to the blender and blitz again to make the shake foamy. Pour into the prepared glasses, top each glass with a second scoop of ice cream and serve immediately with the doughnut skewers.

Popsicles &
SOFT WHIPS

These deliciously pretty popsicles contain plenty of goodness from fresh fruits and exceptionally nutrient-rich beetroot/beet. They are sweetened with coconut flower syrup, which has been used in Thai cooking for generations. It is sticky, so you may need to warm it through before using. It's available from health food or Asian food stores, but date syrup or clear honey are great alternatives.

Beetroot, orange & blueberry
YOGURT POPS

500 g/generous 2 cups Greek yogurt

50 g/1¾ oz. coconut flower syrup (or date syrup or clear honey)

50 g/1¾ oz. raw beetroot/beet, finely grated

50 g/1¾ oz. fresh blueberries

freshly squeezed juice of 1 orange

1 tablespoon icing/confectioners' sugar

6 popsicle moulds and sticks

MAKES 6

Place the yogurt into a bowl and stir in the coconut flower syrup (or other sweetener). Pour the mixture into the six popsicle moulds.

Place the grated beetroot/beet, blueberries and orange juice in a blender and blend until really smooth. Add the icing/confectioners' sugar and blend again. Very carefully drizzle the beetroot/beet syrup into the moulds, swirling each one with a skewer to form ripples through the yogurt.

Add the sticks in an upright position at this stage, or freeze first for a while until the mixture is firm enough to hold the sticks straight. Freeze for 4–6 hours until frozen.

When you are ready to serve, dip the moulds into hot water for a second or two, then gently pull out the popsicles.

Matcha is the finely ground powder of green tea leaves, which are bursting with antioxidants. Here, matcha's earthy flavour marries well with mint and coconut milk for a delicious, healthy and slightly different chilled treat.

MINT CHOCOLATE &
matcha pops

400-ml/14-oz. can coconut milk
4 large fresh mint sprigs, bruised
1–2 teaspoons good-quality
    matcha powder, plus extra
    to serve
4 tablespoons maple syrup
    or clear honey
50 g/1¾ oz. dark chocolate,
    chopped
melted dark chocolate, to serve

6–8 small or 4–6 large popsicle
    moulds and sticks
baking sheet, lined with baking
    parchment

MAKES 6–8 SMALL OR 4–6 LARGE

Combine the coconut milk and mint sprigs in a small pan over a medium heat. Bring the milk just to the boil, then remove from the heat and set aside until cold.

Strain the cold coconut milk, then whisk in the matcha powder and maple syrup (or honey) until completely dissolved. Refrigerate for about 1 hour until set enough to hold the chocolate pieces in place.

Fold the chocolate through the milk and then carefully spoon the mixture into the moulds. Add the sticks in an upright position at this stage, or freeze first for a while until the mixture is firm enough to hold the sticks straight. Freeze for 4–6 hours until frozen.

About 20 minutes before you are ready to serve, put the prepared baking sheet into the freezer.

After 10 minutes, quickly dip the moulds into hot water, then gently pull out the popsicles. Place the popsicles onto the prepared baking sheet and drizzle with melted chocolate. Dust with extra matcha powder and return to the freezer for 10 minutes to set before serving.

All you need is a splash of vodka here and you'd have the perfect frozen daiquiri! But hey, who needs alcohol when you can enjoy this healthier fruit version in the form of a frozen popsicle?

Juicy watermelon &
STRAWBERRY POPS

300 g/10½ oz. strawberries, hulled and halved
3 tablespoons icing/confectioners' sugar, sifted
500 g/1 lb. 2 oz. watermelon
freshly squeezed juice of 1 lemon

8–10 small popsicle moulds and sticks

MAKES 8–10

In a bowl, stir together the strawberries and sugar and leave for 1 hour for the strawberries to release their juices, stirring occasionally.

Cut away the watermelon rind and deseed and roughly dice the flesh.

Place the strawberries and all the juices, the watermelon and lemon juice in a blender and blend until smooth. Divide the mixture between the popsicle moulds.

Add the sticks in an upright position at this stage, or freeze first for a while until the mixture is firm enough to hold the sticks straight. Freeze for 4–6 hours until frozen.

When you are ready to serve, dip the moulds into hot water for a second or two, then gently pull out the popsicles.

Your classic morning breakfast bowl of yogurt, granola, honey and fresh fruit in ice pop form! To be enjoyed at any time.

BREAKFAST GRANOLA
& yogurt pops

60 g/2¼ oz. granola

5 tablespoons clear honey

250 g/generous 1 cup Greek yogurt

150–200 g/5½–7 oz. prepared small fresh fruits such as grapes, strawberries and/or kiwi, peeled and diced

50 g/1¾ oz. frozen or fresh raspberries, thawed if frozen

1 tablespoon icing/confectioners' sugar

6–8 popsicle moulds and sticks
small baking sheet, lined with
*   baking parchment*

MAKES 6–8

Place the granola in a bowl, stir in 2 tablespoons of the honey and mix so that all the granola is really sticky. Divide the mixture between the moulds and press down firmly to compact the granola at the bottom. Freeze for 1 hour until really firm.

Place the yogurt in a bowl and stir in the remaining 3 tablespoons of honey. Spoon a little yogurt mixture into each mould and add some of the fresh fruits, alternating between the two until the moulds are full. Add the sticks in an upright position at this stage, or freeze first for a while until the mixture is firm enough to hold the sticks straight. Freeze for 4–6 hours until frozen.

Meanwhile, purée the raspberries in a blender with the icing/confectioners' sugar, then sieve/strain to remove all the seeds. Refrigerate.

About 20 minutes before you are ready to serve, put the prepared baking sheet into the freezer to chill. After 10 minutes, dip the moulds into hot water for a second or two, then gently pull out the popsicles. Place the popsicles on the prepared chilled baking sheet and immediately drizzle over the raspberry sauce. Return to the freezer for 10 minutes to set before serving.

The name of these says it all. They look really fun and are also great for kids who claim not to like cucumber – offer them one of these frozen treats and watch them change their mind!

Refreshing apple &
CUCUMBER POPS

4 apples
3 Lebanese cucumbers
freshly squeezed juice of 2 limes
100 g/½ cup caster/superfine
   sugar

juicer
6–8 popsicle moulds and sticks

MAKES 6–8

Cut one of the apples in half. Quarter, core and cut one of the halves into wafer-thin slices, reserving the other half. Cut one of the cucumbers in half widthways and then cut one of the halves into wafer-thin slices, reserving the other half. Set all the wafer-thin slices of apple and cucumber aside for a moment.

Pass all the remaining apples and cucumbers and the reserved halves through a juicer. Place the juice in a jug/pitcher and stir in the lime juice and sugar until the sugar has dissolved.

Divide the apple and cucumber slices between the moulds and fill to the top with the cucumber syrup. Add the sticks in an upright position at this stage, or freeze first for a while until the mixture is firm enough to hold the sticks straight. Freeze for 4–6 hours until frozen.

When you are ready to serve, dip the moulds into hot water for a second or two, then gently pull out the popsicles.

Remember 'rockets', those multi-coloured popsicles from your childhood? This homemade version looks great and tastes even better.

Tutti frutti POPS

250 g/1¼ cups caster/white
   granulated sugar
freshly squeezed juice of 2 oranges
freshly squeezed juice of 1 lemon
freshly squeezed juice of 2 limes
125 g/4½ oz. fresh raspberries

8 popsicle moulds and sticks

MAKES 8

Place the sugar in a pan with 500 ml/2 cups water and heat gently, stirring, until the sugar has dissolved. Turn up the heat and boil for 1 minute. Remove the pan from the heat and set aside to cool completely.

Place the orange, lemon and lime juices each in separate bowls and stir enough sugar syrup into each to give approx. 150 ml/⅔ cup liquid per bowl, with leftover syrup. (The exact amount of syrup you add will depend on how much juice your citrus fruits provide.)

Place the raspberries in a blender with 100 ml/⅓ cup plus 1 tablespoon of the remaining sugar syrup. Blend until very smooth. Taste for sweetness and add more syrup if needed.

Pour the orange syrup into each mould to fill about one quarter of the way up. Freeze for about 1 hour until completely set. Pour in the lime layer to fill about halfway up – either add the sticks at this stage or freeze until the mixture is firm enough to hold the sticks. Freeze again until firm and repeat the process, adding then freezing a raspberry layer, then finally adding the lemon layer to fill to the top. Freeze the ice pops for 4–6 hours until frozen.

When ready to serve, quickly dip the moulds into hot water, then pull out the popsicles.

Pretty in pink may well have been the name of an 80s pop song, but it works equally well to describe these delicious and refreshing fruit popsicles. The rosewater marries beautifully with the flavour of the pomegranate and gives it that Middle Eastern-style allure.

Pomegranate, lime &
ROSEWATER POPS

4–5 pomegranates
freshly squeezed juice of 2 limes
30 g/2½ tablespoons caster/white granulated sugar
2 teaspoons rosewater
fresh rose petals, dried rose petals and lime wedges, to decorate (optional)

8 small popsicle moulds and sticks

MAKES 8

Cut the pomegranates in half over a bowl lined with a large sieve/strainer to catch the juices. Set half a pomegranate to one side. For the rest, squeeze out as much of the juice as you can from the seeds, pressing down on them in the sieve/strainer with a metal spoon.

Measure out 500 ml/2 cups of the juice and refrigerate any leftovers for drinking. Stir the lime juice, sugar and rosewater into the pomegranate juice until the sugar has dissolved.

Knock out the seeds from the reserved pomegranate half and divide them between the moulds, then pour in the juice. Add the sticks in an upright position at this stage, or freeze first for a while until the mixture is firm enough to hold the sticks straight. Freeze for 4–6 hours until frozen.

When you are ready to serve, dip the moulds into hot water for a second or two, then gently pull out the popsicles. Decorate with fresh and dried rose petals and lime wedges, if you like.

Indulge in the tropical taste of these layered fruit and coconut popsicles. Bamboo cones lined with baking parchment have been used as moulds, but plastic Champagne glasses are also an excellent idea.

COCONUT, MANGO &
passion fruit pops

100 g/½ cup caster/white
   granulated sugar
1 ripe mango (about 450 g/1 lb.),
   peeled, pitted and flesh diced
1 tablespoon freshly squeezed
   lime juice
200 ml/generous ¾ cup coconut
   cream
200 ml/generous ¾ cup passion
   fruit pulp (from about 6 passion
   fruit)

6–8 popsicle moulds and sticks

MAKES 6–8

Place the sugar in a pan with 250 ml/1 cup water and heat gently, stirring, until the sugar has dissolved. Turn up the heat and boil for 1 minute. Remove from the heat and leave to cool completely.

Place the mango flesh in a blender with the lime juice and blend until smooth. Taste and add a little of the cooled sugar syrup, if necessary.

Whisk together the coconut cream with 1–2 tablespoons of the sugar syrup to your taste. Blend the passion fruit pulp with some of the remaining syrup to your taste.

Divide the passion fruit syrup between the moulds, filling a third of the way up and freeze for about 1 hour until firm. Next, add the coconut cream layer and freeze for about 30 minutes or until the mixture is firm enough to hold the sticks. Press the sticks in gently. Add the mango layer and freeze for a final 2–3 hours until frozen.

When you are ready to serve, dip the moulds into hot water for a second or two, then gently pull out the popsicles.

These frozen treats are an enticing combination of tangy, fresh and sweet. They are sweetened with agave syrup, but honey can also be substituted. Dipping these popsicles into finely chopped pistachios to serve gives a lovely nutty, crunchy finish.

BUTTERMILK, RASPBERRY
& pistachio pops

250 ml/1 cup Greek yogurt
250 ml/1 cup buttermilk
150 ml/⅔ cup agave syrup
125 g/4½ oz. fresh raspberries
25 g/1 oz. unsalted pistachio nuts,
  finely chopped

6 popsicle moulds and sticks

MAKES 6

Put the yogurt, buttermilk and agave syrup in a bowl and whisk together until just combined.

Divide the raspberries evenly between the moulds and then fill them up with the buttermilk mixture.

Add the sticks in an upright position at this stage, or freeze first for a while until the mixture is firm enough to hold the sticks straight. Freeze for 4–6 hours until frozen.

When you are ready to serve, dip the moulds into hot water for a second or two, then gently pull out the popsicles.

Dip the ends of the popsicles in the chopped pistachio nuts to serve.

A rich chocolate mousse coated in dark chocolate topped off with toasted chopped hazelnuts – these are dangerously good!

EXTREME CHOCOLATE
& hazelnut pops

75 g/¾ stick unsalted butter

175 g/6 oz. milk/semisweet chocolate (chips or chopped)

3 eggs, separated

30 g/2½ tablespoons caster/white granulated sugar

200 g/7 oz. dark chocolate, 75% cocoa solids, chopped

25 g/1 oz. hazelnuts, toasted and finely chopped

hand-held electric whisk

6 popsicle moulds and sticks

small baking sheet, lined with baking parchment

MAKES 6

Melt the butter and milk/semisweet chocolate gently together in a small saucepan. Remove from the heat.

Whisk the egg whites with a hand-held electric whisk to stiff peaks, then whisk in the sugar until thick. Beat the egg yolks into the chocolate-butter mix and then fold in the egg whites until just combined. Divide the mixture between the moulds. Add the sticks in an upright position at this stage, or freeze first for a while until the mixture is firm enough to hold the sticks straight. Freeze for 4–6 hours.

About 20 minutes before you are ready to serve, put the prepared baking sheet into the freezer. Meanwhile, combine the chocolate with 50 ml/3½ tablespoons cold water in a pan over a very low heat, stirring until melted and smooth. Let it cool slightly.

After 10 minutes, dip the moulds quickly into hot water, then gently pull out the popsicles. Immediately pour the melted chocolate sauce over the popsicles, coating as much of them as you can. Quickly place the popsicles on the prepared baking sheet and scatter over the hazelnuts. Freeze again for 10 minutes until set before serving.

What else is there to say about this heavenly combination other than make it, then freeze it and eat it – you will not regret it!

SALTED BANOFFEE *pops*

4 tablespoons golden/light corn syrup

1 tablespoon cocoa powder

2 bananas, peeled and chopped

300 ml/1⅓ cups double/heavy cream

25 g/2 tablespoons caster/white granulated sugar

25 g/1 oz. blanched almonds

a little sea salt

4 tablespoons toffee caramel sauce (see page 9)

8 popsicle moulds and sticks

2 small baking sheets, 1 lined with foil and 1 lined with baking parchment

MAKES 8

Place 3 tablespoons of the syrup into a bowl with the cocoa powder and stir well until smooth.

Place the bananas, cream and sugar into a blender and blend until completely smooth. Pour the banana cream into the moulds. Drizzle in the cocoa syrup and swirl through with a skewer to create a ripple effect.

Add the sticks in an upright position at this stage, or freeze first for a while until the mixture is firm enough to hold the sticks straight. Freeze for 4–6 hours until frozen.

Meanwhile, place the almonds and remaining 1 tablespoon syrup in a small frying pan/skillet with 1 tablespoon cold water. Heat gently until the syrup begins to boil. Boil for 3–4 minutes, without stirring, until the almonds are glazed. Transfer the nuts to the foiled baking sheet and sprinkle with the salt. Cool completely, then roughly chop.

About 20 minutes before you are ready to serve, put the paper-lined baking sheet into the freezer. After 10 minutes, dip the moulds quickly into hot water, then gently pull out the popsicles. Place the popsicles on the chilled sheet and drizzle over the caramel. Top with the glazed nuts. Freeze again for 10 minutes to set.

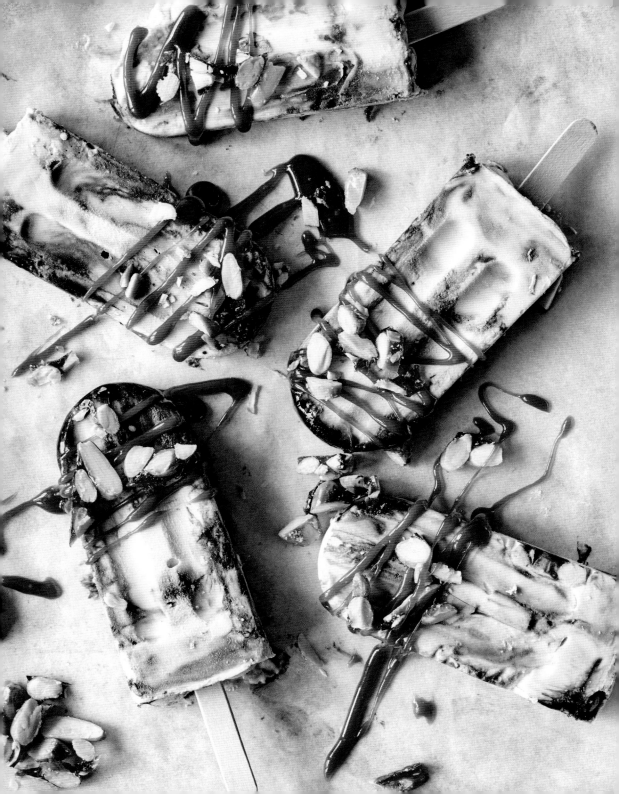

Here almond, coffee and chocolate ice creams are dipped into melted chocolate and coated in crushed Savoiardi cookies. Delicious!

Tiramisù ice cream
POPS

1 tablespoon cocoa powder

1 tablespoon instant espresso coffee powder

2 tablespoons boiling water

250 g/1 cup mascarpone

300 ml/1¼ cups double/heavy cream

50 ml/3½ tablespoons milk

3 tablespoons icing/confectioners' sugar

½ teaspoon almond extract

100 g/3½ oz. dark chocolate, chopped

25 g/1 oz. Savoiardi cookies, crushed

6 small popsicle moulds and sticks

baking sheet, lined with baking parchment

MAKES 6

Dissolve the cocoa powder and the espresso powder separately in 1 tablespoon of boiling water each. Set aside to cool.

Combine the mascarpone, cream, milk, sugar and almond extract in a food processor and blend until smooth. Measure and divide evenly into three bowls. Stir the cocoa mixture into one and the coffee mixture into another, leaving one bowl plain.

Divide the plain cream between the moulds. Freeze for 1 hour or until firm. Add the coffee layer and freeze for 30 minutes or until firm enough to hold the sticks upright. Gently add the sticks and freeze for another 30 minutes until firm. Finally, add the cocoa cream mixture and freeze for 4–6 hours until frozen.

About 20 minutes before you are ready to serve, put the prepared baking sheet into the freezer. Meanwhile, melt the chocolate in a heatproof bowl set over a pan of barely simmering water. Make sure the base of the bowl does not touch the water.

After 10 minutes, dip the moulds quickly into hot water, then gently pull out the popsicles. Immediately dip the ends into the melted chocolate and then into the crushed biscuits/cookies. Place the popsicles on the prepared baking sheet and return to the freezer for 10 minutes to set.

These delectable treats taste like s'mores sandwiched between fresh strawberry ice cream. If you are lucky enough to have any of the toasted marshmallow cream left over, just eat it as it is!

Strawberry & toasted
MARSHMALLOW POPS

300 g/10½ oz. strawberries, hulled and halved
50 g/¼ cup caster/white granulated sugar
200 g/scant 1 cup Greek yogurt
25 g/1 oz. large marshmallows
1 teaspoon vanilla extract
100 ml/⅓ cup plus 1 tablespoon double/heavy cream, whipped until slightly thickened

8 popsicle moulds and sticks
metal skewers

MAKES 8

Dice 50 g/1¾ oz. of the strawberries and reserve for later.

Place the remaining strawberries in a bowl and stir in the sugar. Set aside for 1 hour.

Place the sugared strawberries and their juices in a blender and blend until smooth. Add the yogurt and blend. Divide half the strawberry yogurt between the moulds, reserving and refrigerating the rest. Add the sticks in an upright position, or freeze first until the mixture is firm enough to hold the sticks straight. Freeze for 1 hour until frozen.

Meanwhile, thread the marshmallows onto the skewers and toast over a flame (or under a grill/broiler) until caramelized on the outside but not melted. Set aside to cool, then roughly chop.

Fold the chopped marshmallows, vanilla extract and reserved strawberries into the lightly whipped cream. Divide between the moulds and return to the freezer for about 1 hour until firm. Pour in the remaining strawberry yogurt and freeze for 4–6 hours until completely frozen.

When ready to serve, dip the moulds quickly into hot water, then pull out the popsicles.

Another popular dessert layered in a mould and frozen into popsicle form. Blueberries pair perfectly with lavender and this aromatic floral adds an exotic flourish to an already wickedly good ice pop.

Blueberry & lavender
CHEESECAKE POPS

300 g/1⅓ cups cream cheese
200 ml/generous ¾ cup double/
  heavy cream
freshly squeezed juice of ½ lemon
60 g/⅓ cup minus 1 teaspoon
  caster/white granulated sugar
150 g/5½ oz. fresh blueberries
1 teaspoon edible dried lavender
  flowers
50 g/1¾ oz. speculoos or thin
  ginger cookies
15 g/1 tablespoon butter, melted

8 popsicle moulds and sticks

MAKES 8

Place the cream cheese, cream, lemon juice and half the sugar in a food processor and blend until smooth. Refrigerate.

Place the remaining sugar, the blueberries and lavender flowers in a small pan over a low-medium heat, stirring until the sugar has dissolved. Simmer gently for a further 5 minutes, then let it cool completely.

Divide the cooled blueberry mixture between the moulds. Add the sticks in an upright position, or freeze first for a while until the mixture is firm enough to hold the sticks straight. Freeze for 1 hour or until frozen.

Pour the layer of cream cheese mixture into the moulds and freeze again for 1 hour or until firm.

Meanwhile, put the biscuits/cookies and melted butter in a food processor and blend to fine crumbs. Divide between the moulds and press down. Freeze again for 4–6 hours.

When you are ready to serve, dip the moulds into hot water for a second or two, then gently pull out the popsicles.

Kefir is a cultured, fermented milk drink with a slightly sour, tart taste and the texture of thin yogurt. Kefir is now pretty widely available from health food stores and larger supermarkets, but thick natural/plain yogurt can be substituted here, if you prefer.

Kefir & date SOFT WHIP

750 ml/3¼ cups kefir (pure kefir, rather than the kefir drink)
150 g/5½ oz. pitted and chopped Medjool dates
1–2 teaspoons almond extract, to taste
ice cream cones, to serve (optional)
finely grated dark chocolate, to serve

ice cream machine (optional)
piping/pastry bag with a fluted or plain nozzle/tip (optional)

MAKES APPROX. 900 ML/ SCANT 4 CUPS

Place all the ingredients, except the cones and chocolate, in a blender and blend until completely smooth.

If you have an ice cream machine, use this to churn the mixture according to the manufacturer's instructions. Or, if you are not using a machine, transfer the mixture to a freezerproof container. Freeze for 2 hours, then stir well with a fork to break up the ice crystals. Return to the freezer and continue to stir well every hour until the ice cream is smooth and frozen. It should take about 6 hours in total.

If you want to serve with a very neat finish, then transfer your ice cream to the piping/pastry bag. (If you have used an ice cream machine, then place the filled bag in the freezer for 10 minutes to firm up a bit more.) Pipe the mixture directly into your cones. Alternatively, you can just use an ice cream scoop or spoon.

Serve the cones sprinkled with finely grated chocolate.

This is an amazing dairy-free (and therefore also vegan) ice cream. A little pistachio paste has been added to provide extra colour, but if you can't find any, then just use almond extract as the flavour is very similar.

AVOCADO & PISTACHIO
soft whip

1 large avocado (about 200 g/7 oz.)

500 ml/2 cups plus 2 tablespoons almond milk

60 g/2¼ oz. unsalted shelled pistachio nuts, chopped, plus extra to serve

125 ml/½ cup coconut milk

150 g/⅔ cup agave syrup or clear honey

2 teaspoons pistachio paste or a few drops of almond extract

1 tablespoon freshly squeezed lemon juice

ice cream cones, to serve (optional)

ice cream machine (optional)

MAKES APPROX. 750 ML/3¼ CUPS

Remove the pit from the avocado and scoop the flesh into a blender. Add the almond milk, pistachio nuts, coconut milk, agave syrup (or honey) and either the pistachio paste or almond extract. Blend until really smooth. Add the lemon juice and blend briefly to combine.

If you have an ice cream machine, use this to churn the mixture. Or, if you are not using a machine, transfer the mixture to a freezerproof container. Freeze for 2 hours, then stir very thoroughly with a fork to break up the ice crystals. Return to the freezer and continue to stir well every hour until the ice cream is smooth and frozen. It should take about 6 hours in total.

Spoon the ice cream into serving dishes or cones and sprinkle with extra chopped pistachios to serve.

Buttermilk adds a delicious tang and lightness to ice cream, both in flavour and texture, making it perfect for piping. It is delicious drizzled with this freshly-made (optional) raspberry sauce.

BUTTERMILK
soft whip

500 ml/2 cups plus 2 tablespoons buttermilk
250 ml/1 cup plus 1 tablespoon double/heavy cream
60 ml/¼ cup maple syrup
2 teaspoons vanilla extract
raspberry sauce, to serve (see page 90), (optional)

ice cream machine (optional)
piping/pastry bag with a fluted or plain nozzle/tip (optional)

MAKES APPROX. 750 ML/3¼ CUPS

For the sauce, place the raspberries in a small pan with the maple syrup over a low heat until softened. Turn up the heat and bring to the boil, stirring, until the fruit has broken down. Remove from the heat, then pass the sauce through a sieve/strainer. Leave to cool.

Whisk the buttermilk, cream, syrup and vanilla together until smooth. If you have an ice cream machine, use this to churn the mixture. If you are not using a machine, transfer the mixture to a freezerproof container. Freeze for 2 hours, then stir well with a fork to break up the ice crystals. Return to the freezer and stir every hour until the ice cream is smooth and frozen. It should take about 6 hours in total.

If you want to serve with a neat finish, then transfer your ice cream to the piping/pastry bag. (If you have used an ice cream machine, then place the filled bag in the freezer for 10 minutes to firm up a bit more.) Pipe the ice cream into cups or serving dishes.

Serve drizzled with raspberry sauce, if liked.

Sundaes & SPLITS

This classic combination of sharp raspberries and juicy ripe peaches with a hint of vanilla hardly needs an introduction. It is said to have been invented by the great chef Auguste Escoffier for the soprano Dame Nellie Melba, who loved ice cream but was concerned that the coldness might damage her voice. Escoffier solved this problem by serving the ice cream with fruit to diminish the coldness and in doing so created one of the all-time most popular ice cream desserts.

PEACH MELBA
sundae

4 ripe peaches, stoned and sliced
120 ml/½ cup Amaretto di Saronno liqueur
300 ml/1¼ cups summer berry sauce (see page 9), made with just raspberries
1 quantity vanilla ice cream (see page 8)
200 g/7 oz. fresh raspberries
200 ml/¾ cup double/heavy cream, whipped
12 Amaretti cookies, crushed

RASPBERRY SORBET
350 g/¾ lb. fresh raspberries
100 g/½ cup caster/white granulated sugar
freshly squeezed juice of 1 lemon

ice cream machine (optional)
4 glass sundae dishes

SERVES 4

To make the raspberry sorbet, place the raspberries, sugar and lemon juice in a pan and add 250 ml/1 cup water. Simmer for 10–15 minutes over gentle heat until the sugar has dissolved and the raspberries are soft. Strain the mixture through a fine mesh sieve/strainer to remove the raspberry seeds and leave to cool completely. Churn in an ice cream machine until the sorbet is frozen (or pour the mixture into a freezerproof box and freeze until solid, whisking every 20 minutes to break up the ice crystals).

Place the peach slices in a bowl, pour over the Amaretto and leave the fruit to marinate for about 1 hour.

To assemble, reserve 4 marinated peach slices for decoration and divide the remaining slices between the dishes. Drizzle with a little summer berry sauce. Add a scoop of vanilla ice cream and raspberry sorbet to each dish and add a quarter of the raspberries. Drizzle over some more sauce and top with a second scoop of ice cream. Spoon whipped cream onto each sundae and add the reserved peach slices and the rest of the raspberries. Scatter the crushed Amaretti cookies over the top. Serve immediately.

Pear and ginger is a flavour match made in heaven. Here, juicy pears are poached in ginger wine with bay leaves and honey and served with a refreshing pear sorbet and rich stem ginger ice cream.

Pear & ginger SUNDAE

POACHED PEARS

4 small ripe pears, peeled, stalks intact

2 tablespoons clear honey, plus a little extra to drizzle

a 1-cm/½-inch piece of fresh ginger, peeled

1 bay leaf

1 cinnamon stick

freshly squeezed juice of ½ a lemon

100 ml/3⅓ oz. ginger wine

PEAR SORBET AND TUILES

5 small ripe pears

150 g/¾ cup caster/white granulated sugar

50 ml/1⅔ oz. ginger wine

freshly squeezed juice of 1½ lemons

STEM GINGER ICE CREAM

80 g/3 oz. stem ginger preserved in syrup, finely chopped, plus 2 tablespoons of the ginger syrup

1 quantity vanilla ice cream base (see page 8), chilled

ice cream machine (optional)

baking sheet lined with parchment paper

4 glass sundae dishes

SERVES 4

To make the poached pears, cut the bottom off each pear so that they sit upright. Using an apple corer, remove the core from the base end, leaving the stalks intact. Place the pears in a pan and cover with water. Add all the other ingredients. Simmer, uncovered, for 20–30 minutes until the pears are soft. Leave to cool completely in the poaching liquid then chill in the fridge until needed.

To make the pear sorbet, peel and core 4 of the pears and place them in a pan with 300 ml/1¼ cups water, the sugar, ginger wine and two thirds of the lemon juice. Simmer for 20–25 minutes until the pears are very soft. Allow to cool, then blend with a hand blender to a smooth purée. Churn in an ice cream machine according to the manufacturer's instructions until the sorbet is frozen (or pour the mixture into a freezerproof box and freeze until solid, whisking every 20 minutes to break up ice crystals).

To make the pear tuiles, preheat the oven to 120°C (250°F) Gas ½. Thinly slice the remaining pear. Put the slices on the prepared baking sheet and brush with the remaining lemon juice. Bake in the preheated oven for 2–3 hours, turning half way through cooking, until crisp and slightly translucent.

To make the stem ginger ice cream, stir most of the chopped ginger into the vanilla ice cream base along with the ginger syrup. Churn in an ice cream machine or freeze using the by-hand method on page 6. Freeze until needed.

To assemble, put scoops of ginger ice cream and pear sorbet in the dishes. Top each sundae with a poached pear and decorate with pear tuiles. Drizzle with honey and sprinkle with the reserved stem ginger. Serve immediately.

This cheerful combination of nuts, chocolate, marshmallows and glacé cherries is the perfect pick-me-up for anyone with the blues. Said to have been designed originally to cheer people up in the American depression of the 1920s, this sundae is guaranteed to bring a smile to your face.

Rocky road SUNDAE

MARSHMALLOW ICE CREAM
1 quantity vanilla ice cream base
   (see page 8), chilled
55 g/1 cup mini marshmallows
100 g/½ cup glacé cherries,
   chopped
2 tablespoons toasted coconut
   flakes

CHOCOLATE CRUNCH ICE CREAM
1 quantity chocolate ice cream
   base (see page 8), chilled
6 chocolate cookies, crushed
55 g/⅓ cup salted peanuts

TO FINISH
1 quantity chocolate sauce
   (see page 9)
chocolate vermicelli, to sprinkle
6 halved glacé/candied cherries,
   to decorate

an ice cream machine (optional)
4 glass sundae dishes

SERVES 4

To make the marshmallow ice cream, churn the vanilla ice cream base in an ice cream machine according to the manufacturer's instructions, or freeze using the by-hand method given on page 6. When almost frozen, stir in the marshmallows, cherries and coconut flakes. Freeze until needed.

To make the chocolate crunch ice cream, churn the chocolate ice cream base in an ice cream machine, or freeze using the by-hand method given on page 6. When almost frozen, stir in the crushed chocolate cookies and peanuts. Freeze until needed.

To assemble, put scoops of the marshmallow ice cream in the sundae dishes. Drizzle over some chocolate sauce (warmed if liked) and add a scoop of chocolate crunch ice cream followed by a second scoop of marshmallow ice cream. Sprinkle with chocolate vermicelli and decorate with a few glacé/candied cherries. Serve immediately.

Tangy sharp rhubarb and rich creamy custard is a classic taste combination. Topped with curly rhubarb tuiles, this candy-coloured sundae makes an unusual and fun dessert.

Rhubarb & custard
SUNDAE

RHUBARB SORBET AND TUILES
800 g/1¾ lb. pink rhubarb
freshly squeezed juice of 2 lemons
200 g/1 cup (plus 1 tablespoon extra) caster/white granulated sugar
a few drops of pink food colouring (optional)
1 tablespoon rose syrup

CUSTARD ICE CREAM
500 ml/2 cups ready-made custard sauce
150 ml/⅔ cup double/heavy cream

ice cream machine (optional)
baking sheet, lined with baking parchment
4 glass sundae dishes

SERVES 4

Using a vegetable peeler, peel all the sticks of rhubarb. Thinly slice 2 of the sticks into long strips using the peeler (for the tuiles). Place these in a pan of water with half the lemon juice and the 1 tablespoon sugar. Add a few drops of food colouring, if using. Simmer for 2–3 minutes and then transfer to the prepared baking sheet and leave to dry overnight. Next day twist each strip of rhubarb into a spiral around the handle of a wooden spoon, gently remove and leave to dry in spirals for a further few hours.

To make the rhubarb sorbet, chop the remaining rhubarb into 3-cm/1¼-inch pieces. Place in a pan with 500 ml/2 cups water, the rose syrup and the remaining lemon juice. Simmer for 5–7 minutes over a gentle heat until the rhubarb is soft. Remove one third of the rhubarb and set aside to cool. Simmer the remaining rhubarb for a further 5 minutes until it is really soft. Blitz with a hand blender and churn in an ice cream machine, or freeze using the by-hand method given on page 6. Freeze until needed.

To make the custard ice cream, lightly whisk together the custard and cream. Transfer to an ice cream machine and churn following the manufacturer's instructions, or freeze using the by-hand method given on page 6. Freeze until needed.

Spoon a little custard ice cream into each sundae dish. Divide the poached rhubarb between them, top with some more ice cream and add a ball of rhubarb sorbet. Decorate with the rhubarb tuiles and serve immediately.

If your idea of a perfect summer holiday is lying by an azure-blue swimming pool, sipping a Piña Colada, this is for you! This fun sundae takes all the elements of the popular tropical cocktail – rum, coconut and pineapple – and combines them in a refreshing ice cream sundae. Top with kitsch cocktail umbrellas or similar and your friends won't be able to resist!

HAWAIIAN *sundae*

300 g/10½ oz. fresh pineapple
200 ml/¾ cup coconut-flavoured white rum, such as Malibu
200 ml/¾ cup double/heavy cream, whipped
toasted coconut flakes, to decorate

COCONUT ICE CREAM
3 egg yolks
100 g/½ cup caster/white granulated sugar
400 ml/1⅔ cups coconut milk
200 ml/¾ cup double/heavy cream

PINEAPPLE SORBET
400 g/14 oz. fresh pineapple
100 ml/3⅓ oz. coconut-flavoured white rum, such as Malibu
200 g/1 cup caster/white granulated sugar

ice cream machine (optional)
4 glass sundae dishes
cocktail umbrellas, to decorate (optional)

SERVES 4

To make the coconut ice cream, whisk together the egg yolks with the sugar until they are light and creamy and have doubled in size. Place the coconut milk and the cream in a pan and bring to the boil. Slowly pour the boiled milk over the whisked egg yolks, continuing to whisk all the time. Allow to cool completely. Churn in an ice cream machine, or freeze using the by-hand method on page 6. Freeze until needed.

To prepare the pineapple sorbet, place the pineapple in a blender with 100 ml/3⅓ oz. water, the coconut rum and sugar and blitz to a pulp. Leave to stand for 30 minutes so that the sugar dissolves. Churn in an ice cream machine, or freeze using the by-hand method on page 6. Freeze until needed.

Chop the remaining pineapple into small pieces and soak in the rum for about 30 minutes.

To assemble, divide half of the marinated pineapple between the sundae dishes. Top with a scoop each of coconut ice cream and pineapple sorbet. Cover with the remaining marinated pineapple and then add more ice cream and sorbet. Top each sundae with a quarter of the whipped cream. Decorate with toasted coconut flakes and cocktail umbrellas, if liked. Serve immediately.

There are few more popular ice creams than cookies and cream – it sits at number five in the world ranking of favourite flavours and was the fastest-ever-selling new flavour of ice cream when it was first launched. And it's not difficult to understand why – crunchy cream-filled cookies with rich vanilla and chocolate ice cream is definitely hard to resist.

COOKIES & CREAM
sundae

1 quantity vanilla ice cream (see page 8)

CHOCOLATE COOKIE ICE CREAM
12 regular Oreo cookies, crushed
1 quantity chocolate ice cream base (see page 8), chilled

TO FINISH
3–4 regular Oreo cookies, crumbed
12 mini Oreo cookies
chocolate vermicelli, to sprinkle

ice cream machine (optional)
4 glass sundae dishes

SERVES 4

To make the chocolate cookie ice cream, churn in an ice cream machine, or freeze using the by-hand method on page 6. Just before the ice cream is frozen stir through the crushed Oreo cookies. Freeze until needed.

Layer the chocolate cookie ice cream, vanilla ice cream and cookie crumbs in the sundae dishes. Sprinkle with chocolate vermicelli and decorate with 3 whole mini Oreo cookies or serve them on the side, if preferred. Serve immediately.

Fudgy home-made brownies, chocolate ice cream, coffee ice cream studded with chocolate-covered peanuts and lashings of chocolate sauce make this the ultimate sundae for chocoholics everywhere.

CHOCOLATE BROWNIE
sundae

1 quantity chocolate ice cream
(see page 8)
1 quantity chocolate sauce
(see page 9)

COFFEE ICE CREAM
2 tablespoons instant coffee
1 quantity vanilla ice cream base
(see page 8), chilled
135 g/5 oz. chocolate-covered
peanuts, plus extra to decorate

CHOCOLATE BROWNIES
125 g/9 tablespoons unsalted
butter, melted and cooled
200 g/7 oz. dark/bittersweet
chocolate, melted and cooled
3 eggs
250 g/1¼ cups caster/white
granulated sugar
125 g/1 cup minus 1 tablespoon
plain/all-purpose flour, sifted
100 g/3½ oz. each chopped
macadamia nuts and
chocolate chips

ice cream machine (optional)
20-cm/8-inch square cake pan,
greased
4 glass sundae dishes

SERVES 4

To make the coffee ice cream, dissolve the instant coffee granules in 1 tablespoon of boiling water and leave to cool. Stir the dissolved coffee through the vanilla ice cream base and churn in an ice cream machine, or freeze using the by-hand method on page 6. When the ice cream is almost frozen, stir in the chocolate-covered peanuts. Freeze until needed.

To make the chocolate brownies, preheat the oven to 190°C (375°F) Gas 5. Put the melted butter and chocolate in a bowl and mix. In a separate large bowl, whisk together the eggs and sugar until light, creamy and doubled in volume. Add the flour, melted chocolate and butter mixture, macadamia nuts and chocolate chips to the egg and sugar mixture and fold in with a spatula until the mixture is evenly mixed. Scrape the brownie mixture into the prepared baking pan using a spatula. Bake in the preheated oven for 35–40 minutes, until the brownie has a crust on top but is still soft in the centre. Allow to cool in the tin before transferring to a wire rack to cool completely and cutting into small squares.

Place a square or two of brownie at the base of each sundae dish and top with scoops of chocolate ice cream and coffee ice cream. Drizzle with chocolate sauce and sprinkle with some chocolate-covered peanuts. Serve immediately.

Note You can store any leftover brownies in an airtight container for up to 5 days.

Chocolate and peanut butter make the perfect sweet-and-salty combination. Here peanut butter ice cream is topped with a shard of crunchy peanut brittle and a scoop or two of frozen chocolate yogurt, which cuts through the sweetness to create the perfect sundae for anyone nutty for nuts!

Peanut butter SUNDAE

PEANUT BUTTER ICE CREAM

3 tablespoons crunchy peanut
  butter
1 quantity vanilla ice cream base
  (see page 8), chilled

CHOCOLATE FROZEN YOGURT

2 tablespoons cocoa powder, sifted
2 tablespoons golden/light corn
  syrup
4 tablespoons crunchy peanut
  butter
500 g/2 cups Greek yogurt

PEANUT BRITTLE

85 g/3 oz. salted peanuts
150 g/¾ cup caster/white
  granulated sugar

TO FINISH

1 quantity chocolate sauce
  (see page 9)
250 ml/1 cup double/heavy cream,
  whipped
cocoa powder, to dust

ice cream machine (optional)
baking sheet, lightly greased
4 glass sundae dishes

SERVES 4

To make the peanut butter ice cream, stir the peanut butter into the vanilla ice cream base. Churn in an ice cream machine, or freeze using the by-hand method on page 6. Freeze until needed.

To make the chocolate frozen yogurt, stir the cocoa powder, golden/corn syrup and peanut butter into the yogurt and mix well. Churn in an ice cream machine, or freeze using the by-hand method given on page 6. Freeze until needed.

To make the peanut brittle, sprinkle the peanuts over the prepared baking sheet so that they are close together. Put the sugar in a heavy-based pan and melt over gentle heat. Melt the sugar gently until just golden brown, taking care not to let it burn. Pour the molten sugar over the peanuts, leave to cool and set and then break into shards.

To assemble, layer the chocolate frozen yogurt and peanut butter ice cream in the sundae dishes and drizzle with the chocolate sauce. Top each sundae with a dollop of whipped cream, dust with cocoa powder and decorate with shards of peanut brittle. Serve immediately.

The classic gâteau from the Schwartzwald in Germany is the inspiration for this adults-only sundae. It's a modern update on the 1970s dinner party dessert – moist chocolate cake, cherries, cream and of course the obligatory kirsch liqueur make this sundae a cherry lover's delight.

BLACK FOREST *sundae*

1 quantity chocolate ice cream
   (see page 8)
2 ready-made chocolate muffins,
   cut into cubes
4 tablespoons kirsch
200 g/7 oz. stoned morello
   cherries in syrup
300 ml/1¼ cups double/heavy
   cream, whipped
55 g/2 oz. dark/bittersweet
   chocolate, coarsely grated
4 fresh black cherries, to decorate

CHERRY RIPPLE ICE CREAM
1 quantity vanilla ice cream base
   (see page 8), chilled
4 tablespoons cherry jam/jelly
   or preserve

ice cream machine (optional)
4 glass sundae dishes
a piping/pastry bag fitted with
   a very large star nozzle/tip

SERVES 4

To make the cherry ripple ice cream, churn the vanilla ice cream base in an ice cream machine, or freeze using the by-hand method given on page 6. When the ice cream is almost frozen, add the cherry jam/jelly and stir through gently in swirls so that the ice cream becomes rippled with the jam. Freeze until needed.

To assemble, arrange some cubes of chocolate muffin in the bottom of each sundae dish. Spoon 1 tablespoon of kirsch over each one and divide the morello cherries between the sundae dishes. Top with scoops of cherry ripple ice cream and chocolate ice cream.

Put the whipped cream in the piping/pastry bag and pipe a large swirl on top of each sundae. Sprinkle with grated chocolate and a top with a fresh cherry to decorate. Serve immediately.

This classic sundae is a delectable combination of vanilla ice cream with summer berries and fluffy whipped cream. A tangy strawberry-vanilla sorbet here to give it an extra summery feel, but you could replace it with the Strawberry Ice Cream on page 8 for an even more indulgent treat.

SUMMER BERRY *sundae*

1 quantity vanilla ice cream
   (see page 8)
350 g/12 oz. fresh strawberries,
   hulled and sliced if large
400 g/14 oz. fresh raspberries
1 quantity summer berry sauce
   (see page 9)

STRAWBERRY VANILLA SORBET
450 g/1 lb. fresh strawberries,
   hulled
200 g/1 cup caster/white
   granulated sugar
freshly squeezed juice of 1 lemon
1 vanilla pod/bean, split
   lengthways

TO FINISH
300 ml/1¼ cups double/heavy
   cream, whipped
strawberries, to decorate

ice cream machine (optional)
4 glass sundae dishes

SERVES 4

To make the strawberry vanilla sorbet, chop the strawberries and put them in a pan with 500 ml/2 cups water, the sugar, lemon juice and vanilla pod/bean. Simmer over gentle heat for about 10–15 minutes, until the fruit is very soft. Leave to cool completely and then blitz to a smooth purée with a hand-held blender. Churn in an ice cream machine, or freeze using the by-hand method given on page 6. Freeze until needed.

To assemble, layer the strawberries and raspberries in the sundae glasses with scoops of vanilla ice cream, strawberry vanilla sorbet and summer berry sauce. Top the sundaes with a swirl of whipped cream, and decorate each one with a fresh strawberry. Serve immediately.

Buttery home-made shortcake, juicy fresh strawberries and a rich strawberry and clotted cream ice cream make up this heavenly sundae. If you don't have time to make the shortcake yourself, use a shop-bought cookie instead – Scottish-style petticoat tail shortbreads work well.

Strawberry shortcake SUNDAE

STRAWBERRY AND CLOTTED CREAM ICE CREAM

160 g/¾ cup plus 1 tablespoon caster/white granulated sugar

2 eggs

225 g/scant 1 cup clotted cream

250 ml/1 cup double/heavy cream

250 ml/1 cup whole/full-fat milk

400 g/14 oz. strawberries, chopped

SHORTCAKE

60 g/5 tablespoons caster/white granulated sugar

120 g/9 tablespoons unsalted butter

185 g/1⅓ cups plain/all-purpose flour, sifted

TO FINISH

400 g/14 oz. strawberries, sliced

250 ml/1 cup double/heavy cream, whipped

1 quantity summer berry sauce (see page 9)

ice cream machine (optional)

2 large baking sheets, greased and lined with baking parchment

8-cm/3-inch round cookie cutter

SERVES 4

To make the strawberry and clotted cream ice cream, put the sugar, eggs, clotted cream, cream, milk and strawberries in a blender and blitz for a few minutes until you have a smooth mixture. Churn in an ice cream machine, or freeze using the by-hand method given on page 6. Freeze until needed.

To make the shortcake, preheat the oven to 180°C (350°F) Gas 4. Cream together the sugar and butter and then mix in the flour to form a soft dough, adding a little milk if the mixture is too dry. Wrap the dough in clingfilm/plastic wrap and chill in the fridge for 1 hour. Roll out the dough on a floured work surface to a thickness of about 5 mm/¼ inch. Use the cookie cutter to stamp out 16 rounds. Carefully transfer the rounds to the prepared baking sheets and bake in the preheated oven for 10–12 minutes until golden brown. Leave to cool completely.

To assemble, put a generous layer of sliced strawberries and summer berry sauce in the sundae dishes. Add a scoop of strawberry and clotted cream ice cream, follow with a large dollop of whipped cream and finish with another scoop of the ice cream. Drizzle with the remaining sauce and decorate with a shortcake or serve the biscuits on the side if preferred.

Note You can store any leftover shortcake in an airtight container for up to 5 days.

Lemon meringue pie is one of the world's favourite desserts. The meringue topping shown here was finished off with a cook's blow torch but if you don't have one, buy meringues nests, crush them and sprinkle them over the top of the sundaes.

Lemon meringue pie SUNDAE

LEMON CURD ICE CREAM

2 eggs

225 g/1 scant cup clotted cream

250 ml/1 cup double/heavy cream

250 ml/1 cup whole/full-fat milk

160 g/¾ cup plus 1 tablespoon caster/white granulated sugar

300 g/10½ oz. lemon curd

GIN AND LEMON SORBET

5 unwaxed lemons

100 ml/7 tablespoons dry gin

200 g/1 cup caster/white granulated sugar

MERINGUE TOPPING

2 egg whites

4 tablespoons caster/white granulated sugar

TO FINISH

150 g/5½ oz. digestive biscuits/ graham crackers, crumbed

60 g/4 tablespoons unsalted butter, melted

3 tablespoons white mini marshmallows

100 g /3½ oz. lemon curd

ice cream machine (optional)
4 glass sundae dishes
cook's blow torch (optional)

SERVES 4

To make the lemon curd ice cream, put the eggs, clotted cream, double cream, milk, sugar and lemon curd in a blender and blitz until smooth. Churn in an ice cream machine according, or freeze using the by-hand method given on page 6. Freeze until needed.

To make the gin and lemon sorbet, finely grate the zest from 2 of the lemons and place in a pan with the juice of all 5 lemons. Add the gin, 500 ml/2 cups water and the sugar. Simmer over a gentle heat for 5–10 minutes until the sugar has dissolved and you have a thin lemon syrup. Leave to cool completely, chill and then churn in an ice cream machine, or freeze using the by-hand method on page 6. Freeze until needed.

To assemble, mix together the biscuit crumbs and melted butter and divide between the sundae glasses. Sprinkle in a few mini marshmallows and top with a scoop each of the gin and lemon sorbet and lemon curd ice cream and spoon in some lemon curd. Return the sundaes to the freezer while you make the meringue topping (but only briefly).

To make the meringue topping, put the egg whites in a grease-free bowl and whisk until stiff. Gradually whisk in the sugar 1 tablespoonful at a time until the mixture is very stiff and glossy. Spoon a quarter of the meringue on top of each sundae and brown with a cook's blow torch until the peaks are brown. (Alternatively, sprinkle the top of each sundae with crushed meringue nest.) Serve immediately.

This combination of strawberry, vanilla and chocolate ice creams is a timeless classic. Although ready-made soft scoop Neapolitan ice cream is available to buy, it can't compete with the divine result you get by using your own creamy home-made ice creams and sticky sauces.

NEAPOLITAN
sundae

1 quantity each of vanilla, strawberry and chocolate ice cream (see page 8)
125 ml/8 tablespoons each of summer berry, toffee caramel and chocolate sauce (see page 9)

DECORATED WAFERS
55 g/2 oz. white chocolate
4 large fan wafers
hundreds and thousands/ sprinkles

parchment paper
4 glass sundae dishes

SERVES 4

To make the decorated wafers, break the white chocolate into pieces and place in a heatproof bowl set over a pan of barely simmering water. Heat until the chocolate has melted – it's important that the bottom of the bowl does not touch the water – if it does the chocolate will overheat and spoil. Allow the chocolate to cool slightly and then spoon onto a plate. Roll the top edge of each wafer in the chocolate so that it is thickly coated and then sprinkle with hundreds and thousands. Place the wafers on parchment paper and leave the chocolate to set.

To assemble, spoon a little summer berry sauce into the sundae dishes. Add a scoop of vanilla ice cream followed by a layer of toffee caramel sauce. Next add a scoop of strawberry ice cream followed by a layer of chocolate sauce and top with a scoop of chocolate ice cream. Insert a wafer into the top of each sundae to finish. Serve immediately.

Plump raisins laced with rum, silky smooth rum and raisin ice cream and rich chocolate brownies all come together deliciously to create this indulgent sundae. This is definitely one for the grown-ups!

Rum & raisin
SUNDAE

4 large shop-bought or home-made chocolate brownies (see page 102)

250 ml/1 cup double/heavy cream, whipped

RUM AND RAISIN ICE CREAM

200 g/1½ cups raisins, soaked overnight in 250 ml/1 cup dark rum

1 quantity vanilla ice cream base (see page 8), chilled

150 g/5½ oz. shop-bought rum and raisin fudge, finely chopped

ice cream machine (optional)

4 glass sundae dishes

a piping/pastry bag fitted with a very large star nozzle/tip

SERVES 4

For the rum and raisin ice cream, stir half the rum-soaked raisins into the vanilla ice cream base together with most of the chopped fudge (reserving a little for decoration) and churn in an ice cream machine, or freeze using the by-hand method given on page 6. Freeze until needed.

To assemble, place half a brownie in the bottom of each sundae dish. Spoon over some of the reserved rum-soaked raisins and rum, then top with a scoop of rum and raisin ice cream and a spoonful of whipped cream. Place the remaining brownie halves on top, follow with a further scoop of ice cream and pipe a large swirl of whipped cream on top. Sprinkle over a few rum-soaked raisins and the remaining chopped fudge. Serve immediately.

'Tiramisù' translated from the Italian means 'pick-me-up' and perfectly describes the elements of this dessert – rich strong coffee with a caffeine hit, creamy mascarpone ice cream and the essential dusting of cocoa powder. To make the dessert look like a classic tiramisù, the ice cream needs to be softened slightly when you assemble the sundae. This is best done straight from churning in the ice cream machine or if using the by-hand method, remove from the freezer to soften before use.

Tiramisù
SUNDAE

3 tablespoons instant coffee
   granules
250 ml/1 cup boiling water
150 ml/⅔ cup coffee liqueur
   (such as Tia Maria)
8 Savoiardi cookies
55 g/⅓ cup dark chocolate chips
cocoa powder, for dusting

MASCARPONE ICE CREAM
250 g/1 cup mascarpone cheese
200 ml/scant 1 cup crème fraîche
200 ml/scant 1 cup double/heavy
   cream
2 tablespoons icing/confectioners'
   sugar, sifted

ice cream machine (optional)
4 glass sundae dishes or
   wine glasses

SERVES 4

Dissolve the coffee granules in the boiling water. Add the coffee liqueur and leave to cool completely.

To make the mascarpone ice cream, mix together the mascarpone cheese, crème fraîche and cream and stir in the sugar. Churn in an ice cream machine following the manufacturer's instructions, or freeze using the by-hand method given on page 6.

To assemble, break 4 of the sponge fingers into pieces and arrange them in the bottom of each of the sundae dishes. Drizzle with a little of the coffee liquid until moist. Sprinkle a few chocolate chips over each one and dust with cocoa. Place a spoonful of the softened mascarpone ice cream into each dish and level the surface with the back of a spoon. Arrange the remaining sponge fingers on top and drizzle over a little more of the coffee liquid. Sprinkle with a few more chocolate chips, add a further dusting of cocoa powder and top with the remaining mascarpone ice cream, again levelling the surface with a spoon or pallette knife.

Dust the top of each sundae liberally with cocoa powder and serve immediately.

Mint choc chip ice cream was hugely popular in the 1970s when ice cream flavours were limited and it's easy to understand why, as it's the perfect taste combination. This sundae makes a great end to a dinner party as it allows you to serve your guests 'after dinner' mints as part of the dessert.

Mint choc chip
SUNDAE

MINT SORBET

300 g/1½ cups caster/white granulated sugar

freshly squeezed juice of 1 lemon

20 g/¾ oz. fresh mint, finely chopped

1 teaspoon green food colouring

MINT CHOC CHIP ICE CREAM

1 quantity vanilla ice cream base (see page 8), chilled

1 teaspoon mint essence

100 g/3½ oz. mint chocolate sticks, finely chopped

1 teaspoon green food colouring

MINT CHOC SAUCE

150 g/5½ oz. peppermint fondant-filled chocolate squares (such as After Eights)

250 ml/1 cup double/heavy cream

TO FINISH

4 mint chocolate sticks

ice cream machine (optional)
4 glass sundae dishes

SERVES 4

To make the mint sorbet, put the sugar, lemon juice, fresh mint and green food colouring in a pan with 600 ml/ 2½ cups water. Simmer for 10 minutes until the sugar has dissolved and you have a thin mint syrup. Strain through a fine mesh sieve/strainer to remove the mint and leave to cool. When completely cool, churn in an ice cream machine following the manufacturer's instructions, or freeze using the by-hand method given on page 6. Freeze until needed.

To make the mint choc chip ice cream, add the mint essence, chopped mint chocolate sticks and green food colouring to the vanilla ice cream base and churn in an ice cream machine following the manufacturer's instructions, or freeze using the by-hand method given on page 6. Freeze until needed.

To make the mint choc sauce, place the peppermint squares and cream in a pan and set over gentle heat. Stir until the mints have melted and the sauce is thick and glossy. Leave to cool completely.

To assemble, layer the chocolate mint sauce, mint choc chip ice cream and mint sorbet in the sundae dishes. Decorate each sundae with a mint chocolate stick. Serve immediately.

The grand-daddy of all sundaes – this American classic harks back to the days when bananas were a special treat rather than an everyday fruit. It's the outrageous combination of three sauces and three-flavours of ice cream that makes it so irresistibly over-the-top and totally delicious!

Classic banana
SPLIT

4 large ripe bananas

4 scoops each of vanilla, chocolate and strawberry ice cream (see page 8)

4 tablespoons each of chocolate, toffee caramel and summer berry sauce (see page 9)

TO FINISH

250 ml/1 cup whipping cream, whipped

4 tablespoons chopped mixed nuts

12 glacé/candied cherries, halved

4 fan wafers

ice cream machine (optional)
4 banana split boat dishes

SERVES 4

Peel the bananas and cut them in half lengthways. Arrange split-side up in the dishes. Put 3 scoops of ice cream, in different flavours, down the length of the each banana, between the 2 halves. Drizzle the 3 sauces generously over the top.

Spoon the whipped cream over the ice cream. Sprinkle liberally with chopped nuts and top with glacé/candied cherries. Set the wafers in the ice cream at a jaunty angle, like the sails of a boat. Serve immediately.

HOT RUM AND RAISIN SPLIT

In a variation on the classic, why not try a split made with warm baked bananas? Preheat the oven to 190°C (375°F) Gas 5. Peel 4 bananas and place them in the centre of a large double layer of foil. Carefully pour over half a quantity of toffee caramel sauce (see page 9) and 3 tablespoons dark rum and sprinkle over 3 tablespoons raisins. Fold the foil over the bananas and seal tightly. Place the parcel on a baking sheet and bake in the preheated oven for 15–18 minutes. Let cool slightly, unwrap and then cut in half lengthways and place in banana split boat dishes. Top with scoops of vanilla ice cream (see page 8), swirls of whipped cream and the remaining toffee caramel sauce. Serve immediately.

If you love bananas, this sundae is simply irresistible! In a new twist on the more familiar Banana Split (see page 122), this recipe combines the traditional elements but uses rich banana and vanilla ice creams, toffee caramel and chocolate sauces and is topped with dried banana chips and walnuts. Yum.

$\mathscr{Banoffee}$ SPLIT

4 ripe bananas
1 quantity vanilla ice cream
   (see page 8)
4 tablespoons each of toffee
   caramel sauce and chocolate
   sauce (see page 9)

BANANA ICE CREAM
2 ripe bananas
freshly squeezed juice of 1 lemon
1 quantity vanilla ice cream base
   (see page 8), chilled

TO FINISH
dried banana chips, to sprinkle
chopped walnut halves,
   to sprinkle

ice cream machine (optional)
4 banana split boat dishes

SERVES 4

To make the banana ice cream, put the bananas in a bowl with the lemon juice and use a fork to mash them to a smooth paste. Fold the banana mixture into the vanilla ice cream base and churn in an ice cream machine, or freeze using the by-hand method given on page 6. Freeze until needed.

To assemble, peel the bananas and cut them in half lengthways. Arrange split-side up in the dishes. Put 1 scoop of vanilla ice cream and 2 scoops of banana ice cream down the length of the each banana, between the 2 halves.

Drizzle the toffee caramel sauce and chocolate sauce generously over the top. Sprinkle with banana chips and chopped walnuts to finish. Serve immediately.

The knickerbocker glory is a retro dessert that never really went out of fashion. Who doesn't love a tall sundae glass filled with ice cream, fruit, syrup, wafers and whipped cream? Although not traditional, crushed meringue is included here as well to give an added texture. You can use frozen summer berries as these keep in a handy pack in the freezer so you can make the dessert all year round, but in summer you can use fresh berries. The combination of red fruits is entirely your choice – blackberries, blueberries, strawberries and raspberries all work well.

Knickerbocker GLORY

450 g/1 lb. frozen summer fruits

100 g/½ cup caster/white granulated sugar

½ teaspoon vanilla bean powder or 1 teaspoon pure vanilla extract

4 meringue nests

300 ml/1¼ cups double/heavy cream

8 scoops vanilla ice cream (see page 8)

4 fresh black cherries on stalks, to decorate

4 wafer tubes

4 *large sundae dishes*

SERVES 4

In a saucepan, heat the frozen summer fruits with the sugar and vanilla and simmer for about 10–15 minutes until the fruit is soft and the liquid is syrupy. Set aside and leave to cool completely.

When you are ready to serve, crush the meringues into small pieces. Whip the cream to soft peaks in a clean mixing bowl using an electric mixer or whisk. Layer the cooled fruit compote with some of the cooking syrup with scoops of ice cream, cream and meringue pieces in the sundae glasses.

Top with a spoonful of cream, drizzle over a few more berries and top with a whole cherry. Insert a wafer tube into each sundae and serve immediately. You may not need all of the fruit compote and its juices depending on the size of your glasses.

Ice cream cakes & FROZEN DESSERTS

These ice cream sandwich layer cakes, glistening with a chocolate glaze, make an ideal party treat. You can use any flavour ice cream you like. If you wish, decorate with pretty crystallized rose petals and if you are a fan of rose creams, you could add a little rose extract to the cake batter.

Mini ice cream CAKES

CAKE
225 g/generous 1 cup soft dark brown sugar
225 g/2 sticks butter, softened
4 eggs
150 g/1 cup plus 2 tablespoons self-raising/self-rising flour
30 g/⅓ cup unsweetened cocoa powder
100 g/1 cup ground almonds
2 tablespoons natural/plain yogurt

GLAZE
100 g/3½ oz. dark chocolate, broken into pieces
1 tablespoon golden/light corn syrup
15 g/1 tablespoon butter
100 ml/⅓ cup double/heavy cream
2 heaped tablespoons icing/confectioners' sugar, sifted

TO ASSEMBLE
400 ml/scant 1¾ cups ice cream
crystallized rose petals, to decorate

35 x 25-cm/14 x 10-inch baking pan, greased and lined
6-cm/2½-inch round chef's ring or cookie cutter

MAKES 8 MINI CAKES

Preheat the oven to 180°C (350°F) Gas 4.

In a bowl, whisk together the brown sugar and butter until light and creamy. Add the eggs, one at a time, whisking after each egg is added. Sift in the flour and fold in with the cocoa powder. Fold in the ground almonds and the yogurt. Spoon the mixture into the baking pan and bake in the preheated oven for 25–30 minutes until the cake is firm to touch and a knife comes out clean. Turn the cake out onto a wire rack and leave to cool completely.

When cool, remove the lining paper and place the cake on a chopping board. Using the chef's ring or cookie cutter, cut out 16 circles of cake.

For the glaze, place the chocolate, syrup, butter and cream in a pan and simmer over a gentle heat until the chocolate and butter have melted and you have a smooth glossy sauce. Beat in the icing/confectioners' sugar. Pass the glaze through a fine-mesh sieve/strainer to remove any clumps of sugar.

Place the cakes on a wire rack to cool with a sheet of foil or baking parchment underneath to catch any drips. While the glaze is still hot, pour it over the cakes to cover. Decorate with crystallized rose petals and leave to set.

When you are ready to serve, use the chef's ring or cookie cutter to cut out discs of ice cream the same size as the cakes. It is easiest to bring the ice cream just to room temperature for a few minutes first. Sandwich an ice cream disc between two of the cakes and serve immediately.

On hot summer days there is no nicer treat to serve to kids than ice cream cookie sandwiches. These are made with chocolate, cinnamon and orange – and while the recipe calls for vanilla ice cream, you can substitute chocolate ice cream, cinnamon ice cream or even a layer of orange sorbet in place of one of the ice cream layers.

ICE CREAM COOKIE
sandwiches

COOKIES

350 g/2⅔ cups self-raising/
  self-rising flour, sifted
200 g/1 cup caster/white
  granulated sugar
½ teaspoon bicarbonate of soda/
  baking soda
grated zest of 1 orange
1 teaspoon ground cinnamon
125 g/9 tablespoons butter, plus
  extra for greasing
2 tablespoons golden/light corn
  syrup
1 egg, lightly beaten
200 g/7 oz. dark chocolate,
  chopped into chunks
100 g/⅔ cup white chocolate chips

TO ASSEMBLE

500 ml/2 cups vanilla ice cream
  (see page 8)

*2 baking sheets, lined with silicon
  mats or baking parchment*
*8-cm/3-inch round fluted edge
  cookie cutter*

MAKES 10 COOKIE SANDWICHES

Preheat the oven to 180°C (350°F) Gas 4.

For the cookies, stir together the flour, sugar, bicarbonate of soda/baking soda, orange zest and ground cinnamon in a mixing bowl. Heat the butter with the syrup until the butter has melted, cool slightly and then stir into the dry ingredients with a wooden spoon. Beat in the egg, then fold through the chocolate chunks and chocolate chips.

Place about 20 spoonfuls of the dough on the baking sheets and press down slightly with your fingers. Make sure that you leave gaps between each as the cookies will spread during cooking. Bake in the preheated oven for about 12–15 minutes until the cookies are golden brown. Leave to cool on the baking sheets for about 10 minutes, then transfer to a rack with a spatula to cool.

To serve, press the cookie cutter into the tub of ice cream to make discs of ice cream that are slightly smaller than the size of the cookies and then sandwich between the cookies. (Simply press the cutter into the ice cream and give it a twist and the disc should come out easily.)

Serve each cookie stack straight away as the ice cream will start to melt. It may be easier to wrap the cookie towers in a strip of baking parchment and tie with string to make them easier to eat.

This bombe is such a decadent treat. Using a chocolate sponge roll to line the basin gives the bombe a pretty decorative pattern when you cut into it – a perfect case in which to nestle the chocolate-hazelnut and ice cream layers.

Chocolate & hazelnut BOMBE

GANACHE
50 g/2 oz. dark chocolate
60 ml/¼ cup double/heavy cream
15 g/1 tablespoon butter

CHOCOLATE-HAZELNUT CREAM
250 ml/1 cup double/heavy cream
2 heaped tablespoons Nutella
40 g/1½ oz. chopped roasted
   hazelnuts

SAUCE
100 g/3½ oz. dark chocolate
100 ml/⅓ cup double/heavy cream
2 tablespoons golden/light corn
   syrup
30 g/2 tablespoons butter

TO ASSEMBLE
360 g/12½ oz. chocolate Swiss roll/
   jelly roll
4 scoops store-bought hazelnut
   ice cream, or vanilla ice cream
   (see page 8)
2 meringue nests, crushed into
   small pieces
3 tablespoons toasted chopped
   hazelnuts

*large pudding basin, lined with
   a double layer of clingfilm/
   plastic wrap*

SERVES 8

To make the ganache, in a pan heat the chocolate, cream and butter until you have a smooth sauce. Leave to cool completely. The ganache will thicken as it cools.

For the chocolate-hazelnut cream, place the double/heavy cream and Nutella in a large mixing bowl and whisk until the cream just holds stiff peaks. Stir through the chopped roasted hazelnuts.

To assemble, cut the chocolate Swiss roll/jelly roll into slices and use to line the basin, covering the base and all the sides. When you reach the top of the dish you may need to cut the slices in half so that you can fill the gaps. Place half of the chocolate-hazelnut cream into the basin, then add the ganache followed by a layer of the ice cream. Sprinkle over the crushed meringue and cover with the remaining chocolate-hazelnut cream. Cover the top of the basin with thin slices of any Swiss roll/jelly roll you have left over. Wrap the whole basin in several more layers of clingfilm/plastic wrap and freeze overnight. It is important to work quickly to ensure that the ice cream does not melt.

When you are ready to serve, make the sauce by heating the chocolate, double/heavy cream, golden syrup/light corn syrup and butter in a pan until the chocolate and butter have melted to make a smooth sauce.

Take the ice cream bombe from the freezer and remove the clingfilm/plastic wrap. Place on a serving plate and allow to come to room temperature for a few minutes. Serve cut into slices with the warm chocolate sauce poured over the top and sprinkled with toasted chopped hazelnuts. The bombe will store for up to 1 month in the freezer.

These pies are a classic chocolate whoopie. You'll need to assemble them at the last minute so that the ice cream doesn't melt. You can substitute any flavour of ice cream you like, such as chocolate for a double chocolate treat!

ICE CREAM *whoopie pies*

125 g/9 tablespoons unsalted butter or vegetable shortening, softened
200 g/1 cup dark soft brown sugar
1 egg
1 teaspoon vanilla extract
280 g/2 cups plus 2 tablespoons self-raising/self-rising flour
40 g/⅓ cup cocoa powder
1 teaspoon baking powder
½ teaspoon salt
250 ml/1 cup natural/plain yogurt
100 ml/7 tablespoons hot (not boiling) water

ICE CREAM FILLING
400 g/14 oz. vanilla ice cream in a block
multicoloured sprinkles, to decorate

two 12-hole whoopie pie pans, greased (optional)
8-cm/3-inch round cookie cutter

MAKES 12

Preheat the oven to 180°C (350°F) Gas 4.

To make the pies, cream together the butter and brown sugar in a mixing bowl for 2–3 minutes using an electric hand-held mixer, until light and creamy. Add the egg and vanilla extract and mix again. Sift the flour, cocoa and baking powder into the bowl and add the salt and yogurt. Whisk again until everything is incorporated. Add the hot water and whisk into the mixture.

Put a large spoonful of mixture into each hole in the prepared pans. Leave to stand for 10 minutes, then bake the pies in the preheated oven for 10–12 minutes. Remove the pies from the oven, let cool slightly then turn out onto a wire rack to cool completely.

Shortly before you are ready to serve, remove the ice cream from the freezer and allow to soften slightly. Cut 12 slices each about 2-cm/¾-inch thick and, using the cookie cutter, stamp out a round from each slice. Sandwich an ice cream round between 2 cooled pie halves. Working quickly, put the sprinkles on a flat plate and roll each pie in them so that the ice cream is coated. Serve your whoopie pies immediately with napkins to catch any ice cream drips.

Caramel Alaskas are perfect party pies, with a caramel pastry case, caramel ice cream and toffee sauce. These hot and cold desserts need only one thing – giant forks or spoons to dig in with.

$\mathcal{B}aked$ $\mathcal{A}laska$ PIES

SHORTBREAD
220 g/1⅔ cups plain/all-purpose flour, sifted
a pinch of salt
60 g/5 tablespoons soft dark brown sugar
½ teaspoon vanilla bean powder or 1 teaspoon vanilla extract
150 g/1¼ sticks butter, softened

CARAMEL SAUCE
50 g/¼ cup soft dark brown sugar
50 g/¼ cup caster/white granulated sugar
100 g/7 tablespoons butter
250 ml/generous 1 cup double/heavy cream

ALASKA TOPPING
200 g/1 cup caster/superfine sugar
3 egg whites

TO ASSEMBLE
about 450 ml/15 oz. caramel or toffee ice cream

6 x 10-cm/4-in. loose-bottom, round, fluted tartlet pans, greased
baking beans
piping/pastry bag fitted with a large star nozzle/tip (optional)
chef's blow torch

SERVES 6

For the shortbread, place the flour, salt, sugar and vanilla in a bowl. Mix the butter into the flour mixture to form a soft dough. Press the dough into the pans to go up the sides and base of each pan. Press out thinly with your fingertips. Chill in the fridge for 1 hour.

Preheat the oven to 180°C (350°F) Gas 4. Line the shortbread with baking parchment and fill with baking beans. Bake the shortbread for 20–25 minutes, until golden brown. Leave in the pan to cool, then remove the parchment and beans.

For the caramel sauce, heat the brown and white sugars in a pan with the butter until the sugar has melted. Remove the pan from the heat and cool for a few minutes, then whisk in the cream. Return the pan to the heat and boil gently for a few minutes until the sauce thickens. Leave to cool completely.

When ready to serve, prepare the Alaska topping. Heat the sugar with 60 ml/4 tablespoons of water in a pan and bring to the boil. Whisk the egg whites to stiff peaks and then add the hot sugar syrup in a steady stream, slowly whisking all the time. The hot sugar syrup will cook the eggs. Whisk for 3–5 minutes, until the meringue is stiff.

Working quickly to prevent the ice cream melting, place each pie crust on a serving plate and fill with scoops of the ice cream. Drizzle with a little of the cooled caramel sauce, then spoon or pipe the meringue over the top in swirled peaks. Toast the outside of the meringue with the blow torch until golden brown and caramelized, then serve immediately with the remaining caramel sauce to pour over – either hot or cold.

Pecan pie is an ever-popular American dessert and this recipe is a twist on that classic. This ice cream cake is topped with crunchy pecans and served with a hot toffee sauce which will help the ice cream to melt. Luscious layers of loveliness – get ready to tuck in with a spoon!

Pecan pie ICE CREAM CAKE

CAKE
200 g/7 oz. shelled pecan halves
225 g/2 sticks butter, softened
225 g/generous 1 cup soft dark brown sugar
4 eggs
190 g/1½ cups self-raising/ self-rising flour
1 teaspoon baking powder
1 teaspoon ground cinnamon
1 teaspoon pure vanilla extract or ½ teaspoon vanilla bean powder
2 tablespoons natural/plain yogurt

TOFFEE SAUCE
100 g/½ cup soft dark brown sugar
100 g/7 tablespoons butter
300 ml/1¼ cups double/heavy cream

TO ASSEMBLE
500 ml/2 cups praline-and-cream ice cream or vanilla ice cream (see page 8)

2 x 20-cm/8-inch round cake pans, greased and lined

SERVES 8

Preheat the oven to 180°C (350°F) Gas 4.

For the cake, in a food processor or blender, blitz 60 g/2 oz. of the pecans to very fine crumbs (the texture of ground almonds). In a mixing bowl, whisk together the softened butter and brown sugar until light and creamy. Add the eggs, one at a time, beating after each addition. Sift in the flour, baking powder, cinnamon and vanilla and fold in gently with the ground pecans and yogurt.

Spoon the batter into the prepared cake pans and arrange the remaining whole pecan halves in pretty patterns on top of the cakes. Bake in the preheated oven for 25–30 minutes until the cakes are golden brown and spring back to your touch and a knife comes out clean when inserted into the centre of one of the cakes. Turn the cakes out onto a wire rack to cool and remove the lining paper.

For the toffee sauce, heat the sugar and butter over a gentle heat in a pan until the sugar has dissolved. Add the cream and simmer for a few minutes until the sauce thickens slightly and you have a golden toffee-coloured sauce.

Brush a little of the toffee sauce over the top of the cakes to glaze, using a pastry brush. When you are ready to serve, place one of the cakes on a serving plate. Bring the ice cream to room temperature and place scoops of ice cream over the cake, spreading out in an even layer with a knife. Top with the second cake and then serve immediately with the remaining toffee sauce on the side, reheated if you wish.

This dessert is perfect for anyone who does not like to eat dairy or gluten. Here mango and raspberry sorbets have been used, but the combination is up to you – try lemon and lime work well, or strawberry and lemon.

MERINGUE & FRUIT
sorbet layer cake

MERINGUE

4 egg whites

225 g/generous 1 cup caster/white granulated sugar

1 teaspoon pure vanilla extract

RASPBERRY SORBET

340 g/¾ lb. fresh raspberries

100 g/½ cup caster/white granulated sugar

freshly squeezed juice of 1 lemon

250 ml/1 cup water

MANGO SORBET

4 very ripe mangos, peeled, stoned and flesh chopped

200 g/1 cup caster/white granulated sugar

250 ml/1 cup water

TO ASSEMBLE

icing/confectioners' sugar, for dusting

2 baking sheets, lined with silicon mats or non-stick baking parchment

ice cream machine (optional)

SERVES 8

Preheat the oven to 130°C (250°F) Gas ½. For the meringue, in a mixing bowl, whisk the egg whites to stiff peaks. Add the sugar a spoonful at a time whisking so to make a stiff, glossy meringue. Whisk in the vanilla. Spread the meringue into three circles about 23 cm/9 inches in diameter on the baking sheets (two on one sheet and one on the other). Bake for 1–1½ hours until crisp, set and lightly golden. Leave to cool on the baking sheets.

Gently simmer the raspberry sorbet ingredients in a pan for 10–15 minutes until the sugar has dissolved and the raspberries are soft. Strain through a fine sieve/strainer to remove the seeds and leave to cool. Churn in an ice cream machine according to the manufacturer's instructions until the sorbet is frozen (or pour the mixture into a freezerproof box and freeze until solid, whisking every 20 minutes to break up the ice crystals).

For the mango sorbet, blitz the mango flesh to a smooth paste in a blender. Heat the sugar and water in a pan until the sugar has dissolved and you have a thin syrup. Cool the syrup then add to the blender with the mango purée and blitz again. Churn or freeze the purée as above.

Store the sorbets in the freezer until ready to serve, then bring to room temperature until they are soft enough to scoop. Place one meringue on a serving plate, then add scoops of one sorbet on top. Gently cover with a second meringue. Place scoops of the other sorbet on top and then carefully top with the third meringue. Serve immediately.

Baked Alaska is one of those surprise-inside desserts with a winning combination of hot toasted meringue and chilly ice cream.

BLACKCURRANT
baked Alaska

CAKE

115 g/generous ½ cup caster/white granulated sugar

115 g/1 stick butter, softened

2 eggs

115 g/¾ cup plus 2 tablespoons self-raising/self-rising flour, sifted

1 teaspoon pure vanilla extract

115 g/4 oz. canned blackcurrants in light syrup (drained weight, syrup reserved)

MERINGUE

150 g/¾ cup caster/white granulated sugar

60 ml/¼ cup golden syrup/light corn syrup

125 ml/½ cup blackcurrant syrup (from the canned blackcurrants)

3 egg whites

1 teaspoon pure vanilla extract

TO ASSEMBLE

800 ml/scant 3½ cups blackcurrant ripple ice cream

115 g/4 oz. canned blackcurrants in light syrup (drained weight, syrup reserved)

20-cm/8-inch round cake pan, greased and lined

sugar thermometer

chef's blow torch

SERVES 8

Preheat the oven to 180°C (350°F) Gas 4. For the cake, in a large mixing bowl whisk together the sugar and butter until light and creamy. Add the eggs one at a time, whisking after each one is added. Gently fold in the flour and vanilla. Fold in half of the drained blackcurrants. Spoon the cake batter into the prepared pan and sprinkle over the remaining blackcurrants. Bake for 25–30 minutes until the cake is firm and a knife comes out clean when inserted into the centre of the cake. Turn out onto a rack to cool completely.

For the meringue, simmer the sugar, syrup and blackcurrant syrup until the sugar has dissolved, then bring to the boil. Using a sugar thermometer, heat the syrup to 119°C/238°F (soft-ball stage). In a clean dry bowl, whisk the egg whites to stiff peaks, then add the hot blackcurrant syrup in a small drizzle, whisking continuously, together with the vanilla powder or extract. This is best done with a stand mixer, or if using a hand mixer, have someone else pour in the hot sugar syrup. Whisk for about 10 minutes then leave to cool.

To serve, cut the cake in half horizontally and remove the paper. Place one cake half on a serving plate. Spread a layer of ice cream on top of the cake (the ice cream needs to be softened to room temperature) and sprinkle over half the blackcurrants. Place the second cake on top and pile high with another layer of ice cream and the remaining blackcurrants. Cover the whole cake and ice cream with the meringue, spreading it with a spatula into swirled patterns. It is important that the meringue is cooled before spreading over the ice cream. Toast the meringue with a blow torch and serve immediately.

Coconut and mango make a totally tropical combination. This is a delicate icebox dessert with pretty white and orange layers. The ice cream terrine is coated in a ginger crumb layer which adds a wonderful crunch.

Coconut & mango
ICEBOX TERRINE

COCONUT ICE CREAM

3 UK large/US extra-large egg yolks

100 g/½ cup caster/white granulated sugar

400 ml/scant 1¾ cups coconut milk

200 ml/generous ¾ cup double/ heavy cream

1 large ripe mango, peeled, stoned and sliced into very thin slices using a mandoline or sharp knife

CRUMB LAYER

200 g/7 oz. ginger cookies, blitzed to fine crumbs in a food processor or blender

100 g/7 tablespoons butter, melted and cooled

ice cream machine (optional)

24 x 10-cm/9½ x 4-inch loaf pan, lined with a double layer of clingfilm/plastic wrap

mandoline (optional)

SERVES 8

For the ice cream, in a mixing bowl, whisk together the egg yolks and sugar until very thick and creamy and doubled in size. Place the coconut milk and cream in a pan and bring to the boil. Take off the heat and slowly pour the hot coconut mixture over the whisked egg yolks, whisking all the time. Return the coconut custard to the pan and heat until the custard starts to thicken. Remove from the heat and leave to cool completely.

Churn the cooled coconut custard in the ice cream machine following the manufacturer's instructions (or transfer to a freezerproof container and place in the freezer, whisking every 20 minutes to break up the ice crystals until the ice cream is frozen). Place the loaf pan the freezer to chill.

Spread one-third of the ice cream over the base of the lined loaf pan. Then place a layer of mango on top, using about half of the mango. Repeat with a second ice cream layer and more mango, then finish with the remaining ice cream. Wrap in more clingfilm/plastic wrap and freeze overnight.

To make the crumb layer, stir the biscuits/cookie crumbs through the cooled melted butter, then tip on to a large plate. Remove the ice cream from the freezer and lift out of the pan. Working quickly, peel off the clingfilm/plastic wrap, then press the ice cream loaf into the crumbs so that it is coated all over in a layer of crumbs. Re-line the pan with another double layer of clingfilm/plastic wrap, return the crumbed ice cream to the pan and freeze for a further hour. To serve, remove from the freezer, peel off the clingfilm/ plastic wrap and place on a serving plate. Cut into slices.

This pie is completely kitsch and quirky. You can make it with any flavour of ice cream – or why not try mixing different flavours for a two-tone pie. As the pie contains ice cream it is important to work quickly and place it in the freezer as soon as possible for best results.

ICE CREAM *pie*

PIE CRUST
250 g/9 oz. digestive biscuits/ graham crackers
100 g/7 tablespoons butter, melted

FILLING
500 ml/16 oz. ice cream (flavour of your choosing)
300 ml/1¼ cups double/ heavy cream

TO DECORATE
50 g/2 oz. dark chocolate, melted and cooled
chocolate confections

23-cm/9-in. deep pie dish, greased

SERVES 6

Blitz the digestive biscuits/graham crackers to fine crumbs in a food processor or blender, or place in a clean plastic bag and bash with a rolling pin. Stir in the melted butter, ensuring that all the crumbs are well coated. Press the crumbs into the base and sides of the greased pie dish using the back of a spoon. Place the pie crust in the freezer and chill for 30 minutes. It is important to do this so that the case is cold, which will help prevent the ice cream mixture from melting.

For the filling, bring the ice cream just to room temperature, until it is soft enough to spoon out. Gently whip the double/ heavy cream to soft peaks, then beat in the ice cream quickly. Working very fast, spoon the ice cream mixture into the frozen pie crust and transfer immediately to the freezer. Leave until the filling is frozen completely.

To decorate, drizzle the frozen pie with the cooled melted chocolate and fix chocolate confections on top with a little chocolate. You need to work quickly, as the chocolate will set very quickly on the frozen ice cream. It is also important that the melted chocolate is cooled; if it is drizzled while hot, it will melt the ice cream. Return the pie to the freezer immediately and freeze until you are ready to serve.

When you want to eat the pie, bring it to room temperature and then serve in large slices to your guests. This pie will keep for up to a month, wrapped in clingfilm/plastic wrap, in the freezer.

Fruits of the forest cheesecake is the ultimate 1970s throwback. This version is served in individual portions made in a silicone mould and topped with fresh berries and a drizzle of coulis. If you do not have this shape mould, make the cheesecake in a loaf pan, then cut into slices once frozen. Serve these bars semi-frozen for a twist on a semifreddo-style dessert.

Fruits of the forest
CHEESECAKE BARS

CRUMB BASES

120 g/4 oz. digestive biscuits/
   graham crackers

70 g/5 tablespoons butter, melted

FILLING

300 g/10½ oz. frozen fruits of
   the forest

75 g/scant ½ cup caster/white
   granulated sugar, or to taste

250 g/generous 1 cup mascarpone
   cheese

250 ml/1 cup crème fraîche

250 g/2 cups fresh berries
   (blackberries, raspberries,
   strawberries), for the topping

12-hole silicone cake bar mould
   (each hole 8 x 3 cm/3 x 1½ inches)

MAKES 12

Preheat the oven to 180°C (350°F) Gas 4.

To make the crumb bases, crush the biscuits/graham crackers to fine crumbs in a food processor or place in a clean plastic bag and bash with a rolling pin. Transfer the crumbs to a mixing bowl and stir in the melted butter. Press the buttery crumbs into the base of each hole of the silicone mould firmly using the back of a spoon, then bake in the preheated oven for 10–12 minutes. Leave to cool completely.

For the cheesecake filling, put the fruit and sugar in a pan with 60 ml/¼ cup water and simmer until the mixture is thick and syrupy. Test the berries for sweetness and add a little extra sugar if you wish. Pass through a sieve/strainer to remove the seeds, then leave to cool completely. Reserve a few spoonfuls of this fruit coulis to drizzle over the cheesecakes when serving.

In a large mixing bowl, whisk together the mascarpone and crème fraîche, then fold in the remaining fruit coulis. Taste for sweetness and add a little more sugar if it is not sweet enough. Spoon over the crumb bases in the mould, then transfer to the freezer. Leave until set, then pop the bars of cheesecake out of the mould. Place on serving plates and leave to defrost slightly to soften. Arrange berries on top of each cheesecake and drizzle with the reserved coulis. Serve immediately.

Reminiscent of the kitsch dessert, Arctic Roll, this grown-up version
has pretty lemon layers, all wrapped up in a light citrus sponge.

LEMON MERINGUE *arctic pie*

LEMON SPONGE

4 eggs

115 g/generous ½ cup caster/white granulated sugar

grated zest of 1 lemon

115 g/¾ cup plus 2 tablespoons self-raising/self-rising flour, sifted

1 teaspoon baking powder

LEMON MERINGUE CREAM

300 ml/1¾ cups double/heavy cream

2 heaped tablespoons lemon curd

2 meringue nests, crushed to small pieces

TO ASSEMBLE

4 tablespoons lemon curd

300 ml/1¼ cups lemon sorbet or frozen lemon yogurt, slightly softened

icing/confectioners' sugar, for dusting

1 meringue nest, crushed into small pieces

34 x 30-cm/13 x 12-inch Swiss roll/ jelly roll pan, greased and lined

20 x 12 x 9-cm/8 x 5 x 3½-inch loaf pan, lined with a double layer of clingfilm/plastic wrap

SERVES 8

Preheat the oven to 180°C (350°F) Gas 4. For the sponge, in a large bowl whisk together the eggs, sugar and lemon zest for about 5 minutes using an electric mixer until very thick, creamy and pale. Sift together the flour and baking powder and fold gently into the egg mixture with a spatula, trying not to knock out the air. Spoon into the Swiss roll/jelly roll pan and bake for 15–20 minutes until golden brown and just firm to the touch. Turn the sponge out onto a sheet of baking parchment. Cover with a clean, damp kitchen towel and leave to cool. Remove the towel and lining paper. Trim away the edges of the sponge using a sharp knife.

For the lemon meringue cream, whisk the cream to stiff peaks, then fold through the lemon curd and meringue.

Cut out rectangles of sponge long enough to cover the base and wide sides of the loaf pan. Press into the pan to line, with the sponge a little way above the top on each side. There is no need to put sponge on the short narrow sides.

Spoon half the meringue cream into the sponge case. Spread over 2 tablespoons of lemon curd. Cut the remaining sponge into two rectangles the size of the loaf pan base. Press one rectangle on top of the curd and cover with the lemon sorbet. Cover with the remaining meringue cream. Spread over the remaining lemon curd and top with the second rectangle of sponge. Tightly wrap the cake in clingfilm/plastic wrap and freeze for at least 3 hours.

To serve, remove from the freezer and take off the outer clingfilm/plastic wrap. Use the lining clingfilm/plastic wrap to lift the cake from the pan. and place on a serving plate with the joins on the bottom. Bring to room temperature. Dust with icing/confectioners' sugar, sprinkle on the crushed meringue pieces and serve immediately.

Cashew butter is swirled through this ice cream to give a lovely ripple effect. Drizzle with extra cashew butter to serve, if you like.

Cashew butter
ICE CREAM

180 g/1 cup xylitol
6 egg yolks
400 ml/1¾ cups rice milk
400 ml/1¾ cups soy cream
seeds from 1 vanilla pod/bean
200 g/1 scant cup cashew butter
   (available in supermarkets
   and health food stores)
3 tablespoons agave syrup

ice cream machine (optional)

MAKES APPROX. 1 LITRE/QUART

Put the xylitol and egg yolks in a bowl and, using an electric whisk, whisk until light, fluffy and pale yellow. Set aside for a moment.

Combine the rice milk, soy cream and vanilla seeds in a heavy-based saucepan. Bring to the boil for 1 minute. Remove from heat and cool slightly.

Pour the warm cream mixture into the egg mixture, whisking constantly and vigorously to combine. Pour the mixture back into the pan over a low heat. Using a plastic spatula, stir the mixture constantly in a figure-of-eight motion for 5–10 minutes until thickened. It should be thick enough to coat the back of a spoon.

If you have an ice cream machine, use this to churn the mixture according to the manufacturer's instructions. If you don't have an ice cream machine, pour the mixture into a freezerproof container and freeze. After 30 minutes, remove from the freezer and stir well to break up the ice crystals. Repeat this process at 30-minute intervals until you have a smooth ice cream. It should take about 6 hours.

Mix together the cashew butter and agave syrup and stir through the ice cream to create swirls (save some to drizzle over when serving), then freeze for 30 minutes to fully set.

Frozen yogurt is going through a bit of a renaissance at the moment and it's not hard to see why. Fresh and light with only a fraction of the fat content of ice cream, it is the natural choice for the health-conscious. This recipe, however, is dairy-free as it uses soy yogurt and coconut milk, which is truly delicious.

COCONUT FROZEN YOGURT
with strawberries

700 ml/3¼ cups plain soy yogurt
340 ml/scant 1½ cups coconut milk
100 ml/⅓ cup plus 1 tablespoon agave syrup
2 teaspoons freshly squeezed lemon juice

TO SERVE
fresh strawberries
desiccated/dried shredded coconut, toasted

ice cream machine (optional)

MAKES SCANT 1 LITRE/QUART

Combine the soy yogurt, coconut milk, agave syrup and lemon juice in a bowl and mix until nice and smooth.

If you have an ice cream machine, use this to churn the mixture according to the manufacturer's instructions. Or, if you are not using a machine, pour the mixture into a freezerproof container and freeze. After 30 minutes, remove from the freezer and whisk thoroughly to break up the ice crystals. Return to the freezer and repeat this process every 30 minutes until completely frozen, but not rock hard, as you want to be able to scoop it out easily. It should take about 6 hours.

Scoop the frozen yogurt into serving bowls or a serving dish and top with halved strawberries and desiccated/dried shredded coconut.

INDEX

RECIPE CREDITS

All recipes by **Hannah Miles** (except those listed below) and previously published by Ryland Peters & Small in *Milkshake Bar*, *Sundaes & Splits*, *Layered Desserts*, *Sweetie Pie*, *Cheesecake* and *Whoopie Pies*.

Louise Pickford (previously published by Ryland Peters & Small in *Popsicle Party*)
Pages 54, 57, 58, 61, 62, 65, 66, 69, 70, 73, 74, 77, 79, 81, 82, 85, 86, 154 & 157.

Victoria Glass (previously published by Ryland Peters & Small in *Boozy Shakes*)
Pages 37, 39, 40 & 43.

PICTURE CREDITS

Kate Whitaker
Pages 3, 4, 5, 8, 9, 13, 14, 16–17, 18, 21, 22, 24, 25, 26, 28–29, 30, 31, 33, 34, 35, 36, 44, 45, 46, 47, 48–49, 50, 70, 74, 81, 86, 91, 92, 95, 96, 99, 100, 103, 104, 107, 108, 109, 111, 112, 115, 116, 119, 120, 123, 124 & 125.

Ian Wallace
Pages 55, 56, 59, 60, 63, 64, 67, 68, 71, 72, 75, 76, 79, 80, 81, 83, 84, 87, 155 & 156

Steve Painter
Pages 7, 127, 131, 132, 135, 136, 137, 139, 140, 143, 144, 147, 148, 150, 151, 152 & 157.

Gareth Morgans
Pages 37, 38, 41 & 42.

Claire Winfield
Page 66.

All illustrations by Adobe Stock.

Front cover from right: Alan Yukine; korinoxe; lisagerrard99; StockBURIN; Svetlanas01; lisagerrard99.

Back cover from left: makiaki; Happypictures; nisi; Nataliia Pyzhova; StockBURIN.

1 left betka82; 1 right Happypictures; 11 left betka82; 11 right betka82; 53 left korinoxe; 53 right belokrylowa; 89 left Gstudio; 89 right betka82; 129 left nisi: 129 right EkaterinaP.